Idioms

Published by :
Lotus Press Publishers & Distributors

Idioms

David Copper

Lotus PRESS
4735/22, Prakash Deep Building
Ansari Road, Darya Ganj,
New Delhi - 110002

Lotus Press : Publishers & Distributors
Unit No. 220, 2nd Floor, 4735/22, Prakash Deep Building,
Ansari Road, Darya Ganj, New Delhi- 110002
Ph.: 41325510, 98118-38000
• E-mail : lotuspress1984@gmail.com
www.lotuspress.co.in

Idioms

ISBN: 81-89093-90-8

Printed & Published by : **Lotus Press Publisher & Distributors,** New Delhi-02

Preface

Idiomatic expressions are found in the dialy speech of English people rather than in elaborate, polished compositions. Likewise, on the radio, in novels, newspaper and magazine articles, and books of travel, Idiomatic turns of expression abound.

As as general rule, an idiomatic phrase cannot be altered; no other synonymous word can be substituted for any word in the phrase, and the arrangement of the words can rarely be modified; any attempted change in the wording or collocation will commonly destroy the idom and perhaps render the expression meaningless. Hence, one must be careful to note the precise words that make up any idiom, and also the exact arrangement of these words.

This book is a ready reckoner of common idioms in the English language, with examples and definitions. It is a work of reference which guides the user with simple terms and appropriate usage.

A

ABREAST

To keep abreast of something: be familiar with changes or be acquainted with
Newspapers keep us abreast of the changes in the city.

ABSENCE

Absence of mind: unable to think about one's own actions
His absence of mind has caused the family a lot of problems.

Absence of mind: inattentive or preoccupied
Absence of mind while driving leads to accidents.

ACCOUNT

On account of: owing to
On account of Independence Day the office is closed.

From all accounts: according to all the facts gathered
From all the accounts we got from the employees, they are likely to go on strike.

Take account of: take into consideration.
When we decided to hire him, we had to take into account his inexperience also.

ACE

Ace up one's sleeve: another winner or trump card
Jack has another ace up his sleeve this time to win the match.

ACCORD

Of one's own accord: willingly or voluntarily
She left the organisation of her own accord.

ACHILLES' HEEL

Achilles' heel: A person's vulnerable point
Sam is a kind person, but his Achillese' heel is that he is very generous too.

ACID

Acid test: the ultimate test to prove something right or wrong
The final match will the acid test of our team's capabilities as world beaters.

ACQUIRE

Acquired taste: liking developed after trying the particular thing
Most people dislike bland food, unless you have acquired a taste for it.

ACROSS

Across the board: general rule applied to one and all
Charges of discipline were withdrawn across the board.

Put one across on: trick someone
He planned to put one across on all his colleagues and get a promotion.

ACT

Act up: misbehave, malfunction
My kids act up in a new atmosphere.

Put on an act: fake or pretend to
Though Raj is a coward he puts up an act of bravery.

Catch in the act: discover someone in a particular act
The students were caught in the act of cheating in the exams.

Act the goat: behave foolishly intentionally
All through the party she had been acting the goat to get everyone's attention.

A disappearing act: not to be seen when needed
The children did the disappearing act when they were asked to clean their rooms.

ACTION

In action: functioning, performing
During floods the army will be in action saving thousands of lives.

Man of action: one who is active and energetic
Our soldiers have to be men of action.

ADAM

Adam's ale: water
I prefer the Adam's ale to any other drink to quench my thirst.

Not know someone from Adam: have no knowledge of someone's existence
He spoke to me at length though I don't know him from Adam.

ADD

Add to: aggrevate or intensify
To add to her misfortune she had to sell all her jewellery.

Add insult to injury: increase the intensity of an existing problem
We had a heavy downpour—an added insult to injury when it was flooded already.

ADMIT

Admit to something: confess, or reveal the mistake
He had to admit his crimes in front of the jury.

ADVANTAGE

Take advantage of: selfish movtive, gain
We took advantage of the bright sunshine to visit the beach.

AEGIS

Under the aegis of: patronage or sponsorship of
The meeting is being held under the aegis of the state government.

Under the aegis of: with the support of
The meetings were held under the aegis of the state government.

Be afraid of one's shadow: a timid person.
Since she was very meek, she was afraid of her own shadow.

AFTER

Aftermath: effects or results
He is still recovering from the aftermath of chickenpox.

Look after: manage
It is our duty to look after our elders.

After one's heart: according to one's wish
It is very difficult to find a mate after one's heart.

Hanker after: look for eagerly
The child was hankering after its mother's attention when she was busy making her career.

AGE

Come of age: mature, grow up
Lily can decide for herself as she has come of age.

For ages: duration, for years
It has been ages since we have corresponded.

AGREE

Agree to/upon/for/on: accept or approve of
We had to agree upon the final rate for the quotation.

AID

In aid of: help or assistance
Our country donated lakhs of rupees in aid of the famine victims.

AIR

Put on airs: pretend to be superior
Ever since her excellent results she is putting on airs.

Clear the air: clear nagging doubts
Though we did not come to an agreement, we cleared the air on different issues.

Cut the air with a knife: sense an ill feeling or resentment
When the manager walked into the office, everyone stared at him; you could have cut the air with a knife.

Airs and graces: behave haughtily
His airs and graces have made him a very unpopular candidate for the elections.

Alice in wonderland: an imaginary world filled with illogical and insane inhabitants
After her wedding, she felt like Alice in Wonderland at her in-laws' house.

ALIVE

Alive and kicking: very much active
Though my grandma is nearing 70 she is alive and kicking.

ALL

All in all: totally or wholly
All in all the programme was a great success.

All along: always
He knew he loved her all along.

All agog: excitedly
We were all agog when the actor walked up to us and spoke a few words.

All moonshine: very unreal
The promises he made before marriage were all moonshine and she was in for a shock.

ANCHOR

Cast anchor: stop or rest on
After a hectic tour of the North we decided to cast anchor before continuing our journey.

ANGEL

An angel of mercy: someone who is comforting and merciful
When I lost my wallet, he came like an angel of mercy and helped me reach home safely.

On the side of angels: agreeable to the normal ways of thinking
She will never get into trouble as she is on the side of the angels.

ANSWER

Answer back: retort or refute
Jack's teacher was angry when he answered back in front of the whole class.

Answer to the description: relate to the description given
This photograph answers to the description of the lost boy.

ANVIL

Upon the anvil: on the agenda
The proposal for construction of another building is upon the anvil in today's general body meeting.

ANYTHING

Anything but: not acceptable
The food at the new restaurant was anthing but satisfactory.

APE

Ape: copy or mimic
We are trying to ape the west in our way of thinking.

APPEARANCE

Put in an appearance turning up or attend
The busy actor put in an appearance at the inauguration of the show.

Keep up appearances: maintain an outward show of wealth and prosperity
They had to keep up appearances, so they decided to buy an expensive car.

APPETITE

Whet one's appetite: sharpen one's desires
The aroma from the kitchen really whetted our appetite for lunch.

APPLE

An apple of discord: cause for disharmony or misunderstanding
The property was the apple of discord between the brothers.

In apple pie order: very neat and tidy
The children arranged their rooms in apple pie order to please their parents.

Upset the apple cart: upset or disrupt smooth running of something
The break-down of our vehicle upset the apple cart of our tour of the country.

APRON

Tied to someone's apron: be dependent on
She is tied to her mother's apron and does not want to leave the house.

ARCH

Arch enemy: foremost rival
The Pandavas and Kauravas were arch enemies.

ARGUE

Argue the toss: disagree on certain issues
At the interview he argued the toss regarding his salary and did not get the job.

ARM

Arm with: equip or supply
The thief attacked the bank armed with a sten gun.

With open arms: eagerly accept
The king welcomed the poet with open arms.

Keep at arms length: discourage
Jack always kept his relatives at arms length.

Chance one's arm: take risks
He decided to chance his arm and invest in the shares.

Armchair theory: suggestion not based on experience
The armchair theory suggested by the new manager was unacceptable to the staff.

Armed to the teeth: fully armed
We were armed to the teeth before we embarked on the journey.

ARTICLE

Article of faith: staunch belief
Foresight is an article of faith with the old lady.

AS

As against: opposite to
As against the wishes of the teacher the children were very noisy.

As and when: whenever needed
We went shopping for grocery as and when we required it.

ASHES

Lie in ashes: destroy completely by burning
The monuments lay in ashes as the army tried to salvage the remains.

AT

At a stretch: continuously
We had to watch two movies at a stretch.

At the eleventh hour: at the last minute
It is not advisable to study your syllabus in the eleventh hour.

At sixes and sevens: confused or disorderly
The books are at sixes and sevens at the new library.

ATTACK

Blunt the attack: weaken the attack of an opponent
Her presentation of the facts blunted the attack on her superiors.

AVAIL

Of no avail: of no consequence or use
Tom tried to persuade his friend but to no avail.

AXE

Get the axe: fired or dismissed
She got the axe from her employer for being careless.

B

BABE

A babe in arms: helpless person or a small child
She felt like a babe in arms in the company of her city friends.

BACK

At the back of one's mind: a thought that is there but not a priority
He tried to recollect the lesson which was there at the back of his mind for some time now.

Back to front: reversal
Jack was trying to read the book back to front.

Back away: retreat in fear
We had to back away when the dog attacked us.

Back up: confirm or support
All scientific theses need a back-up of proved documents.

Behind one's back: on the sly
Gossiping is a pastime done behind one's back.

Get off my back: to be left alone
Please get off my back and let me think clearly for a while.

Put on the back burner: postpone work for later
All the suggestions were put on the back burner when the chairman made the rules.

Back the wrong horse: support the loser
The fact that she was a novice was evident when she backed the wrong horse.

With one's back to the wall: no win or desperate situation
By the end of three months the army was fighting with their backs to the wall to save the country.

BACKBONE

Have no backbone: not have integrity
The financial dealing is in a mess as he is a man without backbone.

BAD

Bad blood: ill feeling
There is so much bad blood among the two countries.

Bad debts: loans that cannot be recovered
The government decided to waive off the bad debts of the farmers.

From bad to worse: situation getting more critical or grave
After the elections the country's progress has gone from bad to worse.

Bend over backwards: go out of the way.
He had to bend over backwards to woo her in style.

BALANCE

Hang in the balance: not sure or uncertain
The committee's decision regarding the CEO nominations is hanging in the balance.

Throw off balance: be in danger of falling
They were shaken off their balance when the building collapsed.

BALL

Have a ball: having fun or enjoyment
When the lecturer did on come the students decided to have a ball.

Have the ball in one's court: be answerable to the present situation
After the general body meeting the ball was in the manager's court to take the next step of action.

Have the ball at one's feet: be in a position to become successful
All his efforts have been successful. He has the ball at his feet.

On the ball: alert and fast
We were able to finish all the assignments on time as we were on the ball throughout the year.

BALLOON

When the balloon goes up: critical situation
As a responsible manager it is his duty to be at the helm when the balloon goes up.

BANANAS

Go bananas: go crazy or wild
He will go bananas if he finds out that his desk has been searched.

BANG

Be bang on: be right on target or correct
She was bang on time to catch the school bus.

BANK

Break the bank: leave one penniless
It won't break the bank if we indulge in a little luxury.

BAR

Behind bars: jailed or in prison
He has to be put behind bars for his crime.

BARE

Bare one's heart /soul: share your innermost feeling
He could only bare his heart to his mother.

BARGAIN

Strike a bargain: make a deal
We had to make a bargain with the sales person for buying goods in bulk.

BARGEPOLE

Not touch with a bargepole: not wish to be associated with one
Uncouth people like him should not be touched with a bargepole.

BASE

Make first base: complete the basic proceedings
We decided to make first base with the project before our manager returned.

BASH

Have a bash at: try
I still want to have a bash at swimming in a river.

BAT

Blind as a bat: fully blind
She is blind as a bat without her glasses.

Not bat an eyelid: not seeming surprised or tensed
He did not bat an eyelid when the doctor told him of his disease.

Have bats in the belfry: be a little insane
All my colleagues think that I have bats in the belfry.

BATTLE

Half the battle: initial step in accomplishing a difficult task
We have found a tenant for our new house, that is half the battle won.

Fight a losing battle: trying to win a difficult war
The Naxalites are fighting a losing battle with the army.

BE

Be all and end all: goal
The be all and end all reason for the riot was to destabilise the government.

Be oneself: act naturally
In order to have a successful relationship one has to be oneself all the time.

BEAD

Draw a bead upon: aim at something
In a fit of anger she drew a bead at the man and threw the knife at him.

BEAM

On the beam: positive approach
He was on the beam while dealing with the little boy.

Broad in the beam: wide in the hips
She was a beauty though she was broad in the beam.

BEAN

Know how many beans make five: know how to look after oneself
Teenagers these days know early in life how many beans make five.

BEAR

Bear in mind: be considerate
While dealing with outlaws we have to bear in mind their backgrounds.

Lose one's bearing: lose control of one's actions
As age catches up we tend to lose our bearing.

Bear fruit: give results
His patience and perseverance has borne fruits after 25 years.

Bear the brunt: suffer the consequences
We have to bear the brunt of the teacher's anger for the incompletion of the project.

A bear garden: a noisy get-together
Their parties are always a bear garden.

Bear the palm: be victorious
He was focused on his studies throughout the year and bore the palm of the exams.

BEAT

Beat around the bush: being indirect
Instead of beating around the bush please tell me the truth regarding the investigation.

Beat the daylights out: thrash or beat up
He beat the daylights out of his son for stealing money.

Beat the clock: finish before time
My daughter always beats the clock in finishing her home-work.

BECK

At someone's beck and call: wait to be ordered around
The teacher had all the students at her beck and call.

BEG

Beg to differ: not agree
She thinks that he is the smartest but I beg to differ.

Beg pardon: request
I beg your pardon, but could you repeat your name please?

BEGIN

To begin with: start off with
To begin with, let us first study about our country.

BEHALF

On behalf of: representing
On behalf of the team I wish you all the very best.

BEHEST

At one's behest: at one's wish or order
The thief carried out the attack at the behest of the Don.

BEHIND

Behind bars: in prison or in jail
He was put behind bars for all his crimes.

Behind closed doors: secretly
Their financial dealings are always behind closed doors.

Behind the scenes: without the knowledge of others
The appointments were made behind the scenes.

BELIEF

To the best of my belief: to the best of my knowledge
To the best of my belief he is innocent.

BELIEVE

Believe in: trust in
She had to believe in the man she was going to marry.

Believe it or not: it is odd but it is different.
Believe it or not I had the same dream last night.

BELL

Ring a bell: sounds familiar or recognizable.
The name rings a bell but I can't figure out where I have met her.

Sound as a bell: being very healthy
Though she is touching eighty, her health is sound as a bell.

BELT

Hit below the belt: injustice or unfair proceedings
He was hit below the belt by his boss when he was due for a promotion.

Tighten one's belt: live below one's standard due to circumstances
Due to the loss in business, he was forced to tighten his belt and live ordinarily.

BEND

Bend the rules: relax the rules to suit one's needs
The government decided to bend the rules when the offender was a minister's son.

Bend over backwards: go out of the way to please someone
The new bride bent over backwards to please her stern mother-in-law.

Bent upon: determined about
He is bent upon studying medicine though he cannot afford it.

BEST

Best bet: result-oriented action/plan
Your best bet would be to vote for the ruling party.

Make best use of: use something to the best of their advantage.
She made best use of her looks to attract the male members of the office.

At one's best: in the best form
Sam was at his best during the interview.

Put one's best foot forward: to the best of one's ability
At the theatre festival she put her best foot forward and got a standing ovation.

Best of both worlds: benefit of two different situations.
Earning in a foreign land gave him the best of both worlds as he could come back to his country anytime.

BET

Hedge one's bet: protect oneself
The rules may change anytime now, it is better to hedge one's bet and play safe.

BETTER

Better safe than sorry: it is better to be cautious than repent later
It is better to get health checkups yearly after the age of 40; it is better to be safe than sorry.

Better late than never: do what is needed even though you are late
Send her a birthday card though her birthday was last week; its better to be late than never.

Be better off without: be happier without
We are better off without his intervention.

BIG

Big shot: influential person
He got admission in the college since his father is a big shot.

Give a big hand: applaud / praise
The audience gave a big hand when she performed on stage for the first time.

BILL

Foot the bill: pay another person's bill
Jack footed the bill for his brother's birthday party.

Fit the bill: meet the requirements
This candidate will surely fit the bill because of his qualifications.

BIRD

The bird has flown: wanted person has escaped
The bird has flown from its secure hiding place.
Kill two birds with one stone: with one effort get two results or answers
He killed two birds with one stone when he combined his business trip with his holiday.

An early bird: an early entrant or riser
He is an early bird always on time for work.

The bird and the bees: sex education
Before entering their teens children these days have to be told about the birds and bees.

BIT

Do one's bit: share the work
If we want good results in the school all teachers will have to do their bit.

Bit by bit: piece by piece
To go on that dream holiday he had to save bit by bit.

Bits and bobs: small objects
Her purse is always filled with bits and bobs.

Take the bit between the teeth: be determined to solve a problem
When her son failed in the examination, she took the bit between her teeth and prepared to teach him at home.

Bits and bobs: small trinkets or little objects
Her handbag is full of bits and bobs.

BITE

Bite one's tongue: trying no to be too honest or frank; be remorseful
After the heated argument with his boss he bit his tongue in remorse.

Be bitten by: have strong liking or interest in
He is bitten by the movie bug and plans to see one every week.

Bite the dust: fail or have a mighty fall
The king fought bravely but had to bite the dust in the hands of the enemy.

Once bitten twice shy: once lost, the second time wary of the same thing
She was deserted by the boyfriend and now she says once bitten twice shy in love.

BLACK

Black and blue: hurt very badly
The thieves beat him black and blue and ran away with the booty.

In black and white: written or printed
I need the agreement in black and white.

BLAME

Lay the blame: make someone the scapegoat.
In the banking scam, the blame was laid on the manager who was innocent.

BLAZE

Blaze a trail: be a pioneer
He blazed a trail by becoming the first millionaire of the country.

BLESSED

Be blessed with: lucky with
She is blessed with a beautiful voice.

BLESSING

A blessing in disguise: an improper situation turning into a fortunate one
I wanted to avoid the function; it rained so heavily that it was a blessing in disguise.

Count one's blessings: be thankful for one's good fortune than complain about what one does not have
When I see a handicapped person I count my blessings that I am all right.

BLIND

Blind as a bat: not able to see clearly
In twilight she is blind as a bat.

Turn a blind eye: ignore
She was beautiful, so her friends turned a blind eye to her character.

Blind drunk: stupor or very drunk
When the party members were blind drunk the hotel manager doubled their bills.

The blind leading the blind: one inexperienced person leading another
The blind leading the blind will only add to the existing confusion.

BLINK

Blink the fact that: ignore
You can't blink the fact that he is a con man.

BLOOD

Be out for someone's blood: seek revenge
She was out for his blood as he had deserted her after their affair.

In cold blood: intentionally /heartlessly
He murdered the man in cold blood.

Blood is thicker than water: family comes first before anyone.
She stood up for her son though he was wrong, after all blood is thicker than water.

Bad blood between: enmity or dislike
There is so much bad blood between the two neighbours.

Getting blood out of a stone: impossible to obtain from someone
Trying to get her to repay the loan is like getting blood out of stone.

BLOW

Blow hot and cold: to be interested and disinterested in turns
She blows hot and cold, so it is difficult for him to gauge if she really likes him.

Blow one's trumpet: boast about oneself
The manager is so unpopular because he is always blowing his own trumpet.

Blow one's top: lose temper/get angry
When the teacher found that the students had not completed the assignment she blew her top.

Blow by blow account: report in detail
The passers-by gave a blow by blow account of the accident.

BLUE

Blue-eyed boy: favoured person
As he was the blue-eyed boy of the manager his mistakes were ignored.

Once in a bluemoon: rarely
The son visited his parents in their old age home once in a bluemoon.

Out of the blue: suddenly
Out of the blue it started raining cats and dogs.

BOAT

Be in the same boat: be in the same situation as others
We have to pay the same amount of taxes as the businessmen; all of us are sailing in the same boat.

Miss the boat: miss an important opportunity
She applied for the job a bit too late and missed the boat.

BODY

Keep body and soul together: support life
After he died his family is struggling to keep body and soul.

Over my dead body: to express strong resentment
You can marry my daughter over my dead body.

Body and soul: wholly or completely
She was in love with him body and soul.

BOLT

Make a bolt for it: to wriggle out of a situation fast
When they realised that the people would find out about the fraud they made a bolt to another country.

A bolt from the blue: sudden turn of events
The maharaja's death came like a bolt from the blue to his subjects.

BONE

Bone of contention: a reason for disagreements and arguments
The division of ancestral property is the bone of contention between the three brothers.

Make no bones about: feel no hesitation
She hated the sight of him and made no bones in showing it.

To the bone: fully or thoroughly
He was cheated to the bone by his friends.

Close to the bone: revealing the truth mercilessly
The investigator was able to find out all the truth about her past close to the bone.

BOOKS

By the book: follow rules strictly
He follows the principles set by his predecessors by the book.

A closed book: completely unknown subject
Before I started working computers was a closed book to me.

An open book: easily understood subject
His life is like an open book, so easy to follow.

Read someone like a book: know a person completely

She can never tell a lie and get away with it for I can read her like a book.

Be in someone's good / bad books: be in and out of favour with someone

Jack was in the bad books of all his teachers because he was a big prankster.

BOOT

Lick someone's boots: praise or flatter to gain a favour

To climb up the corporate ladder he licked the boots of his bosses.

Get too big for one's boots: act high and mighty

Once she got the post in the council she was acting too big for her boots.

Tough as an old boot: very strong

The injury did not lay him down as he is tough as an old boot.

To boot: along with or added to

He is rich and spoilt to boot.

The boot is on the other foot: reversed situation

It was his wife who misled the family and not the other way about; the boot is on the other foot.

BORN

Born and bred: lived and grown up in a particular place

She was born and bred in London.

A born fool: who is foolish from the beginning

She is always getting into trouble for she is a born fool.

Born with a silver spoon in the mouth: belonging to an affluent or rich family

He does not have to worry about his saving money as he is born with a silver spoon in his mouth.

Born in the purple: born in a royal family

His mannerism and stature shows that he is born in the purple.

BOTTOM

From the bottom of one's heart: truly or sincerely

The old man thanked me from the bottom of his heart for saving him from the accident.

Be at the bottom of: be the cause of

Sam was the culprit; he is at the bottom of all the confusion.

Get to the bottom of: find out the truth

The detective was bent upon getting to the bottom of the murder trial.

BOW

Have two strings to one's bow: have a second or alternative skill or resource.
As both a teacher and a businessman, he has two strings to his bow.

BRAIN

Have something on the brain: keep thinking constantly
This misunderstanding has been on my brain for the past one week.

Brain-drain: loss of learned experts to another country
The brain-drain in our country is due to the lack of academic facility available for research.

Rack one's brain: exert one's mind greatly
I had to rack my brain before I could solve this problem.

BREAD

A bread and butter letter: a letter thanking for one's hospitality
When we returned after a good holiday, we wrote a bread and butter letter to our host for a wonderful stay.

BREADTH

Length and breadth: throughout
We walked for five hours through the length and breadth of the forest.

By a hair's breadth: very narrowly
She escaped the fall from the stairs by a hair's breadth.

BREATH

Catch one's breath: gasp
The sight of the Himalayas made us catch our breath.

Out of breath: panting
I was out of breath when I went jogging this morning after so many years.

A breath of fresh air: refreshing change
In the monotonous office, listening to my radio was like a breath of fresh air.

BRIGHT

A bright spark: active or lively
Children are the bright sparks of every household.

Bright and early: at the crack of dawn
On the day of school picnic children are up bright and early.

The bright lights: city life
She was lured by the bright lights of Bombay.

BRING

Bring to light: discover
He brought to light the defects of the old system.

Bring home: show beyond doubt
After their world cup win the Indian team brought home the winning streak.

BROAD

In broad daylight: during the day
The murder took place in broad daylight.

BROKE

Stony broke: have no money or penniless
He is always stony broke at the end of the month as he is a big spendthrift.

BUCK

The buck stops here: responsibility is accepted and not passed on
Let the buck stop here, the blame cannot be shifted to all the staff.

Pass the buck: shift the responsibility
Everytime there is a big project she passes on the buck to someone else so that she can be free.

BUNDLE

Bundle of nerves: tensed or anxious
I am a bundle of nerves every time an exam is approaching.

BULL

A bull in a china shop: destructive or crude
He is like a bull in a china shop amidst the people in his office.

Take the bull by the horns: go forward to deal with a problem without fear
She took the bull by the horns and asked her boss for a better workplace.

BUNCH

A bunch of malarkey: an untrue story
His story was a bunch of malarkey to the judge's ears.

BURN

Burn the midnight oil: study very hard
Instead of burning the midnight oil during the exams its better to start preparing earlier.

BURY

Bury the hatchet: patch up the differences.
Its better to bury the hatchet and become friends than sulk in loneliness.

BUS

Miss the bus: lose an opportunity or chance
The applications were issued last week itself, and so she missed the bus coming today.

BUSH

Beat about the bush: not being clear about
Stop beating about the bush and tell me the correct answer.

BUSY

Busy as a bee: very busy
She has no time for small talk she is always busy as a bee.

BUT

But then: on the other hand
She is the right candidate for the job but then she can't work on the computers.

BUZZ

Give a buzz: make a phone call
She gave a buzz to the hospital and fixed an appointment.

BYGONES

Let bygones be bygones: let us forget and forgive
The two families let bygones be bygones and met each other after fifteen years.

C

CACKLE

Cut the cackle: stop talking unimportant things
Cut the cackle and come to the point about what you have to say!

CAKE

Take the cake: take away all the glory
We knew he was an idiot but this move of his takes the cake.

A piece of cake: an easy task
The maths paper was a piece of cake for him

Cakes and ale: the good things in life
His aim was to have cakes and ale all through his life.

CALCULATE

A calculated risk: risk taken with known dangers
We have to take a calculated risk when we invest in shares

CALL

Be on call: available whenever necessary
My job in the school is only on call.

Call one's bluff: challenging a person to carry out his threats
Every word he utters is filled with lies and so I decided to call his bluff.

Call it a day: quit or stop
After being in the film industry for so long she decided to call it a day after her marriage.

Call it quits: stop a contest or duel on equal terms
When the opponents started losing they conveniently decided to call it quits.

Call the shots: be in control
Ever since she became the manager she has the power to call the shots.

CAN

A can of worms: complicated problem
What seemed to be a simple task turned out to be a can of worms.

CANTER

An easy canter: an easy victory without much effort
He won the match in an easy canter as his opponents were weak.

CAP

Cap in hand: modestly
The rich man donated money to the orphanage with a cap in hand.

To cap it all: to give finishing touches to
He was a topper throughout the year, and to cap it all he won a university rank.

A feather in one's cap: a thing of pride
The team's victory was like a feather in the cap of the captain

CAPER

Cut a caper: act foolishly
When the children were told that the holidays were extended they cut a caper.

CARD

Strongest card: best argument
Her strongest card was that she was better than all the other candidates present for the interview.

Trump card: strong point/winner
Her looks were her trump card to win the college elections.

Play one's card right: take advantage of the situation
He played his cards right and became the president of the company.

Put one's cards on the table: reveal the correct position
I have put my cards on the table, this is the only way I can repay your debt.

Get one's cards: get dismissed or fired
When he was caught taking a bribe, he got a card from his management.

CARE

Care of somebody: in the custody or guardianship of somebody
When he went abroad he left his aged mother in the care of his aunt.

Take care that: be careful
Take care that you don't drive fast when you have had a few drinks.

CARPET

On the carpet: called to be reprimanded
The principal called the boys on the carpet for the unrest they created in the college.

Sweep something under the carpet: try to forget something unpleasant.
She tried to make a new beginning with her life by sweeping her past under the carpet.

CARRY

Carry the can: accept the blame or responsibility
When he was grilled by the police, he carried the can.

CART

Put the cart before the horse: do things in the reverse or wrong order
Isn't it rather putting the cart before the horse to paint the house when we are planning to change the flooring?

CASE

As the case may be: depending on the situation
Whether or not we should travel at night will be decided in the evening, as the case may be.

In any case: in the event of any happenings
In any case you are going to miss the train, so take your time to pack.

Just in case: possibility of something happening
Carry the umbrellas in the car just in case its starts raining.

In that case: if at all
We hear that there is a traffic jam; in that case we will take another route.

CAST

Cast one's eye: examine something quickly
He cast his eye on the audience before beginning his speech.

Cast a spell: magical power
The wizard cast a spell on the old lady.

Cast one's vote: elect or give one's choice
In order to cast one's vote one has to be eighteen years and above in age.

Cast one's mind back to: remember the past
If you cast your mind back to your childhood, it will make you feel pleasant all over again.

CASTLE

Castles in the air: weaving a dream that may never come true
The poor farmer built castles in the air about becoming rich.

CAT

Lead a cat and dog life: life full of quarrels
In spite of living a cat and dog life they celebrated their golden wedding anniversary.

Let the cat out of the bag: divulge a secret.
We wanted to keep his results a surprise but his nosy neighbour let the cat out of the bag.

Curiosity killed the cat: excessive inquisitiveness can be troublesome.
Her over enthusiasm to reach her goal led to her fall; too much curiosity killed the cat.

Rain cats and dogs: rain heavily
Last month it rained cats and dogs in our district.

Like a cat on hot bricks: being nervous or restless
I felt like a cat on hot bricks, when I had to face the interview.

No room to swing a cat: very little space
The rooms in this apartment are so small,there's no room to swing a cat.

Put the cat among pigeons: introduce something that will cause more trouble.
They have introduced maths to the Arts students which will put the cat among pigeons.

CATCH

Catch one's attention: attract someone
At the party he was trying his best to catch the attention of the pretty girl.

Catch one's breath: stop breathing due to shock.
We caught our breath at the mere sight of the mighty Himalayas.

Catch fire: burn
The forest caught fire due to the negligence of the officials.

Catch one napping: find someone disinterested
The young children in the audience were caught napping during the speech.

Catch one on the wrong foot: catch someone unexpectedly
The girl was caught on the wrong foot with evidence when she tried to cheat the boy.

Catch a glimpse of: have a fleeting sight of
I caught a glimpse of the boy whom she was going to marry.

Catch 22: no win situation
It was a catch 22 situation for our teams in the final match.

CAUTION

Throw caution to the winds: act recklessly without thinking about the consequences
The robbers threw caution to the winds and went about looting the bank.

CAVIARE

Be caviare to the general: be too refined for the ordinary people
When she returned from the finishing school, she was a caviare to the general.

CHANCE

By any chance: a possibility
By any chance do you have some extra money on you?

By chance: accidentally
When I was walking on the road I came across a 100 rupee note by chance.

Chances are that: it is likely that
The chances are that they will all do well in the exams.

No chance: not likely at all
There is no chance of rains this month.

Take a chance on: try something though odds are against us
Though the opposition is sure of victory, let us take a chance on the young man and vote for him.

Take chances: take risks
It is not wise to take chances with shares when your finances are not sound.

CHANGE

Change hands: pass on to another person
This family heirloom has changed many hands before coming back to our family.

Change one's mind: change one's decision
After much thought on this matter I have changed my mind.

Change places with: exchange positions
We have to change places with our parents to understand their agony.

For a change: vary one's routines
We went out for dinner for a change.

CHASE

A wild goose chase: look for something that is hard to find.
We went on a wild goose chase to look for the house with the misleading address.

CHEAP

Go cheap: low priced
The sweaters in the supermarket are going cheap this summer.

Hold something cheap: something which you hold with less value or esteem
We hold ostentatious living cheap and not worthwhile.

Put a cheat upon: dupe or swindle
By putting a cheat upon us she lost a place in our hearts.

CHEEK

Turn the other cheek: react to an attack in a mild manner
By turning the other cheek, he taught a lesson to all the others who were bent upon revenge.

Cheek by jowl: uncomfortably close
The rich man now lives in an apartment, cheek by jowl with the ordinary folks.

CHEW

Chew the cud: think about something
When he was told about the losses incurred, he chewed the cud in a very slow manner.

Chew the fat: whine or grumble

When the kids were told that they were not allowed to the concert, they chewed the fat for a long time.

CHILD

Child's play: easy task
The maths puzzle was a child's play for him.

Be with child: be pregnant
She is with a child for the third time.

CHINK

Chink in the armour: a weakness in a person that makes him an easy target for an attack
He found a chink in her armour when he spoke about her children.

CHILL

Chill one to the bone: become very cold or freeze
Though we were in the snow for only a few minutes we were chilled to the bone.

CHIP

A chip off the old block: having the same traits as one's parents.
He was a spendthrift like his dad, a real chip off the old block.

When the chips are down: when times are down.
When the chips are down we tend to lean towards God.

CHORD

Strike a chord: reminder
That face strikes a chord. We must have met before.

CHUCK

Chuck it: stop immediately
We are bored of hearing your chatter, just chuck it!

CIRCLE

A vicious circle: related events
These days people are caught up in the vicious circle of making money, then spending money and then working for more money.

Come full circle: come back to the beginning
He started as a mechanic, rose to a high position, squandered money and has come back full circle to being a mechanic again.

CIRCUMSTANCES

Under the circumstances: in the present situation
Under the circumstances it is better he stays in the hospital for further investigation.

CLAPPERS

Like the clappers: fast or quick
Work like the clappers.

CLEAN

A clean sheet: new beginning
After the bad experience she wanted to start her life with a clean sheet.

Come clean: confess the truth
She kept denying the truth until the priest spoke to her, she then decided to come clean.

CLEAR

Clear the decks: remove obstacles
We had to clear the deck for the new management takeover.

Make oneself clear: express oneself clearly.
When I hired the new maid I made myself very clear and told her what was expected of her.

Stay/steer clear of something: avoid something
We decided to steer clear of our dirty neighbour.

CLEFT

Be caught in a cleft stick: in an indecisive situation
Now that she had to decide between her work and home she was caught in a cleft stick.

CLOCK

Round the clock: without stopping
To complete the given assignments, she has been working round the clock.

Put the clock back: go back in time
At the reunion all of us decided to put the clock back and have a good time.

CLOSE

At close quarters: very near
I witnessed the accident at very close quarters.

A close shave: a situation in which you just manage to escape
In the hit and run accident she had a close shave with only a few bruises.

Keep a close watch: watch something very intently
We had to keep a close watch on the quotations lest it would leak from the office.

Lie close: hide
The thief lay close in the bush till night and then broke into the house.

Close a deal: make a business agreement
After examining all the facts we closed the deal with the multinational firm.

Draw to a close: conclude or end
As the concert drew to a close the audience screamed for more.

COAT

Cut one's coat according to one's cloth: live according to one's means
After the loss in business, it was difficult for him to live according to his coat.

Hang on to someone's coat tails: become successful by associating oneself with persons who are successful
She realised that if she has to get a promotion, she has to hang on to the manager's coat tails.

COIN

Coin it/money: make money easily
He always wanted to coin money easily without working hard for it.

Pay back in the same coin: tit for tat
She decided to pay back her detractors in the same coin by going to court.

COLD

Get cold feet: lose courage in the last minute
As the date for elections were approaching near, she got cold feet and withdrew her nominations.

Give someone a cold shoulder: ignore someone
At the party he was conceited enough to give his friends a cold shoulder.

Leave someone in the cold: neglect someone
We were left in the cold when we were given the wrong directions to their house.

In cold blood: mercilessly
The thief murdered the old woman in cold blood and ran off with her booty.

COLOUR

One's true colours: real character
We saw her true colours when she did not win the contest.

With flying colours: highly successful
She was elated that she passed the exams with flying colours.

Lend colour to: make something more realistic
He is such a good actor that he lends colour to any role he plays.

COME

Come again: please repeat
Come again? I'm sorry I could not hear you.

Come easily: naturally
He is such a fraud, lying comes easily to him.

Come what may: whatever may happen
I have to finish this assignment today, come what may.

To come: in future
We will have many natural calamities in the months to come.

COMPANY

The company one keeps: the kind of people one moves with
You are known with the company you keep.

For company: escort
At the party we had a whole lot of kids for company.

Get into/keep bad company: association with undesirable people
We have to teach our children to avoid bad company.

CONCLUSION

In conclusion: in the end
In conclusion I'd like to say that it is better to be late than never.

Jump to conclusion: assume with knowing the facts
Don't jump to conclusions about their relationship, I am sure it is a platonic one.

CONSIDERATION

In consideration of: on account of
In consideration of his capabilities the company has decided to promote him.

Take something into consideration: review
When we plan a picnic we have to take the weather into consideration.

CONTROL

Be in control: reign or control
The English were in control of the whole country because our kings were not united.

Bring under control: be in charge or dominate
Even during severe oppression the government was able to bring the situation under control within a week.

COOL

Keep/lose one's cool: be in control of one's composure
Even though he was provoked at the meeting he kept his cool and answered all the questions calmly.

Cool as a cucumber: be very calm whatever the situation is
During all the turbulent times he has been cool as a cucumber.

Cool one's heels: keep waiting
As the police kept running around for clues to the murder the accused had to cool his heels in prison.

CORN

Tread on someone's corn: hurt one's feelings
Her boss is a big boor and enjoys treading on everyone's corn.

CORNER

Corner of one's eye: catch a glimpse quickly
He caught sight of the beautiful girl from the corner of his eyes.

Just around the corner: close by
Summer vacation is just round the corner.

Cut corners: do a task in an easy way
By cutting corners we will not be able to do a perfect job.

CORRIDOR

Corridors of power: governmental departments where important decisions are taken
Once he won the local elections, he decided that he had to aim and get into the corridors of power.

COST

At all costs: whatever situation arises
At all costs he must be stopped from going to court tomorrow.

At the cost of: at the loss of
She had to go to work at the cost of her health.

COUNSEL

A counsel of perfection: a perfect advice which is difficult to follow
The advice that I got from my grandmother was a counsel of perfection.

Keep one's own counsel: keeping one's opinions a secret
Though she knew that her husband was wrong, she kept her own counsel.

COUNT

Count one's blessings: be grateful for what one has
We have to count our blessings before being dissatisfied with everything that we have.

Count one's chickens (before they are hatched): overconfidence about success
Before you get the money in your hands don't count your chickens for anything can happen.

COURSE

In course: at the appropriate time
In course of time she will be able to grasp the language.

A course of action: planned procedure
We have to first plan a course of action before getting involved in the project.

In course of time: sooner or later
She has to face the music for her action in course of time.

COVER

Cover one's tracks: leave no evidence.
The terrorists had covered their tracks so well that they had a very easy way to escape.

CRACK

The crack of dawn: early in the morning
We embarked on our journey at the crack of dawn.

Get cracking: move fast
We have to get cracking and finish the project within one month.

CRADLE

From cradle to grave: from birth to death
She has lived a full life from cradle to grave.

CRAMP

Cramp one's style: come in the way of or hinder one's style.
The new rules laid down in the office cramped the style of the employees.

CREST

On the crest of a wave: in the height of success or fame
After his consecutive wins he is riding on the crest of a wave.

CROSS

Cross one's path: hold up
He never forgives anyone who crosses his path.

At crossroads: at a point where decisions have to be made
I am at crossroads whether to marry him or not.

Cross one's finger: hope for the best
I crossed my fingers hoping that my son would perform well in his exams.

Cross swords with: argue or disagree with someone
He was always crossing swords with his boss.

Cross one's palm with silver: give a coin
I crossed the doorman's palm with a silver before he let me inside the auditorium.

CRY

In full cry: in eager pursuit
The team began practice in full cry before the final match.

Cry over spilt milk: regret or be remorseful
After the loss there is no use crying over spilt milk, for we played badly.

Cry one's heart out: sob uncontrollably
The old woman cried her heart out on the death of her son.

CURRY

Curry favour: gain a favour by flattery or praise
He curried favour with the boss before he got the promotion.

CUSHY

A cushy number: an easy job or life
All these rich brats have a cushy number.

CUSS

Not give a cuss about: not be worried at all, don't care a damn
I do not give a cuss about what you people think of my idea.

CUT

A cut above: better than others
She is a cut above all the students in academics.

Be cut out for: be best suited for
He sings beautifully, and he is cut out to be a playback singer.

D

DAB

A dab hand: very skilled
He is a dab hand at managing all the mechanics in our factory.

DAILY

One's daily bread: food
We all work hard for our daily bread.

One's daily dozen: routine exercises
One's daily dozen always keeps one fit.

DAMN

I'm damned if: I will surely do
I 'm damned if I let her get away with this kind of work.

Give a damn: do not care
I give a damn about who I have to meet.

DAMSEL

Damsel in distress: lady who is in trouble
He loves to help any damsel in distress.

DANCE

Dance to one's tune: act according to one's wishes
The little boy had everyone dancing to his tune.

DARK

Before/after dark: before/after sunset
She wanted to reach home before dark.

Keep it dark: keep in secrecy
He was planning to go abroad but wanted to keep it dark till he got his visa.

A dark horse: someone who is not too familiar
The French team was the dark horse but they walked away with the cup.

In the dark: ignorant
We were kept completely in the dark about his movements.

DAY

By day/night: during daytime/after dark
She worked by day and studied at night.

Day by day: as time goes by
Day by day his illness is causing a lot of alarm.

One's days are numbered: one is going to die soon
He made his will when he knew that his days were numbered.

In this day and age: nowadays
In this day and age who believes in arranged marriages?

One of these days: very soon
One of these days he is going to be promoted to the post of a manager.

The other day: recently
I spoke to your parents the other day.

Those were the days: recollection of happier times
Those were the days when roads were devoid of congestion.

To this day: even today
To this day he cycles to his place of work.

Day in, day out: every day without ceasing
He had to slog for a decent living day in, day out.

Call it a day: retire from work
He decided to call it a day when his health started failing.

Make someone's day: make someone happy
The child's day was made when his father came back home from work early.

DEAD

A dead end: final point
We were at a dead end when there was no way to ease the situation.

Over my dead body: vehemently oppose something
You will marry this girl over my dead body.

Dead against: opposed to
I am dead against him becoming the chief minister.

In the dead of night: middle of the night
He reached home in the dead of night.

Dead beat: very tired
After a hard day at the field the farmer was dead beat.

Dead to the world: in deep slumber
They were so dead to the world that they did not hear the thief enter their house.

DEAL

Great deal: a lot.
He has a great deal of respect for her.

Deal one a blow: cause a setback
She dealt a blow when she resigned at a crucial time.

Raw deal: unjust dealings
He was given a raw deal when his junior was made the boss.

DEATH

Put one to death: kill someone
For the crime he committed he was put to death by law.

To the death: until one is dead
It was a fast to the death till the demands were met.

At death's door: on the verge of death
He was at death's door when he saw that his family was happy.

DEBT

Be in and out of debt: owe or not owe money
He was in debt for most of his life as he was a spendthrift.

Run into debt: when a person owes a lot of money
He has run into a debt to the tune of lakhs of rupees with his bankers.

DEEP

Deep down: in reality or underneath the surface
She seems very casual but deep down she is a tensed person.

In deep waters: in trouble
When he lost his passport he found himself in deep waters.

DELIGHT

Take delight in: find joy in
He takes great delight in teasing all the girls.

DEMAND

In demand: popular
A sincere worker is always in demand.

On demand: as requested
She was sent on demand to work for another department.

DEPTH

In depth: thoroughly
We went through the article in depth but found no information we wanted.

DESIGN

Be designed for: planned for a purpose
The door is designed for better appearance.

Have designs on something/someone: plan to get someone or something
He had designs on the manager's chair and decided to get it somehow.

DEVIL

Go to the devil: be damned
Go to the devil! We are better off without you.

Give the devil his due: give the person you detest a fair chance
He was a very mean fellow, but to give the devil his due he had a soft corner towards my son.

Talk of the devil: someone who makes an appearance as he is talked about.
Talk of the devil and here he comes.

The devil's own luck: getting very lucky
He has to have the devil's own luck to get such a hike in his salary.

DIE

Die hard: rigid or immovable
He is a die hard Gandhian.

Never say die: never give up
Never say die to any failures.

DIG

Dig one's own grave: be a cause for one's own failures or downfall
By lying to the manager she dug her own grave.

DIRTY

A dirty look: a look of disapproval
I gave the man a dirty look when he was ogling at all the women at the bus stop.

DISAPPEARING

Disappearing act: be absent when needed most
When it was his turn to go up on stage, he did a disappearing act.

DISTANCE

In the distance: far away
We saw the twinkling stars in the distance.

Keep one's distance: be aloof
Though the neighbourhood was friendly, she kept a distance.

Keep one at a distance: does not get too familiar with
He always kept his relatives at a distance.

DO

It won't do: not satisfactory
Just completing the assignment won't do, you have to present it properly.

Nothing doing: refusal
Nothing doing, you cannot go out this evening.

That does it: used to show that someone cannot be pushed any further.
That does it! I am not prepared to tolerate your attitude any longer.

That will do: an expression used to stop an argument.
That will do, I will not listen to your lies anymore.

Do's and don't's: rules and regulations
If you follow the do's and don't's of the club, you will not have any problem.

DOG

A dog in the manger: not allowing a person from having or doing something which he himself cannot have.
He is a dog in the manger, he owns a big car but does not let his family use it.

Let sleeping dogs lie: do not stir up trouble

Let sleeping dogs lie, please do not fight with the neighbour.

Go to the dogs: spoiled or ruined
The factory has gone to the dogs with his mismanagement.

Teach an old dog new tricks: learn new things during old age
Learning computers at the age of seventy-five was like teaching an old dog new tricks.

In the doghouse: in shame or disgrace
After the calamity the family is now in the doghouse.

Lead a dog's life: lead an unhappy life
I was leading a dog's life until I met him.

DONKEY

Donkey's years: a very long time
Its been donkey's years since we had so much fun.

Talk the hind leg off the donkey: talk too much
By talking the hind leg off the donkey, she always gets herself into trouble.

DOUBLE

In double harness: with the help of a partner or spouse
They were able to finish the project fast in double harness.

At the double: very fast
They arrived for the concert on the double.

DOUBT

Beyond any doubt: surely
I know I can trust him beyond any doubt.

In doubt: unresolved or uncertain
The decision of the CEO is still in doubt.

No doubt: assuredly or it is likely that
No doubt he has good intentions but he comes across as a liar.

DOWN

Down below: below in a basement or beneath
The iron chest is hidden down below in the basement.

Go down with: fall ill with
After the trip to the hills he went down with a bad virus.

Down and out: condition after a loss of money and home
After the auction of his house he is down and out.

DRAW

Draw one's attention: engage or bring to one's notice
She brought to my attention the torn dress I was wearing.

Draw a blank: no response or no answer
After searching for four hours we drew a blank and could not find the house.

Slow on the draw: slow to understand
She is always slow on the draw and takes a very long time to finish the task given to her.

Draw a parallel between: compare or find contrast with another
We have to draw a parallel between the two candidates before we choose one.

DRINK

Be the worse for drink: drunk
He comes home everyday the worse for a drink.

Drink to somebody's health: toast to someone's well being.
After the success of the project, we all drank to the health of the staff.

Drink like a fish: drink large quantities of alcohol
This small bottle of beer is not enough for him, he drinks like a fish.

DROP

Drop dead: collapse
She dropped dead at the site of her injured son.

Drop a hint: give a clue tactfully
She dropped a hint to her fiancée that she might call off the engagement.

Drop in a line: write a letter.
I dropped in a line to him informing of the change in address.

Drop names: use names of influential or powerful people to impress others
By dropping a few names her father was associated with she got the contract.

At the drop of a hat: frequently.
He fell in and out of love at the drop of a hat.

DRY

Dry as dust: drab or dull
His presentation at the seminar was dry as dust.

Milk someone dry: use someone to the fullest

The second wife milked him dry of all his resources and left him for another man.

DUCK

Play ducks and drakes with something: spend foolishly
He played ducks and drakes with his fortunes and lost everything.

Water off a duck's back: have no effect or impression
Talking about morals to him is like water off a duck's back, we only waste our energy!

Take to something like a duck to water: easily adaptable
He took to swimming like a duck to water within four days.

Like a dying duck: act weakly or pathetically
She was sick last month but even now behaves like a dying duck.

DUE

In due course: at the appropriate time
He will understand me in due course.

Give somebody his due: give someone credit
He is not popular among the students, but give him his due as he is very knowledgeable.

DUDGEON

In high dudgeon: being offended
He walked out of the meeting in high dudgeon

DUMPS

Down in the dumps: dejected
She is down in the dumps as she failed in the exams.

DUST

Kick up a dust: create a commotion, disturbance.
The groom's party kicked up a dust over the marriage arrangements.

Bite the dust: fail or be unsuccessful
The company was badly mismanaged and the share holders bit the dust.

E

EARS

Be all ears: listen attentively
The whole family was all ears when the will was read out to them.

Reaches one's ears: hears the news or gossip
When the news of the election reaches his ear he will host a party.

Within earshot: within hearing distance
She was within earshot when the girls were talking about her.

Lend an ear: heed or listen
At the time of need only his friends lent an ear to his problems.

Turn a deaf ear: refuse to listen
She turned a deaf ear to the problems of her children.

EARLY

Bright and early: an early riser
Bright and early is the only motto for success.

Early days yet: too premature
We do not know if this relationship will last, it is early days yet.

The early hours: very early in the morning
He goes partying till the early hours of the day.

EARTH

How on earth: possibility
How on earth did he find his way in the forest?

Bring one down to earth: take a practical look at life

She brought him down to earth and explained the disadvantages of the new money scheme.

Move heaven and earth: do everything humanly possible to achieve one's goal.
He moved heaven and earth to get a seat in the prestigious college.

EARTHLY

No earthly use: without any use
It is no earthly use his coming in so late to work.

Not having an earthly: very less chance or hope
When asked about finding the loot, he said he did not have an earthly.

EASE

Stand at ease: stand with feet apart and hands behind
The soldiers stood at ease and listened to the minister's address.

Feel at ease: soothing and comfortable
We felt at ease in her house.

Ill at ease: feel awkward in the presence of someone
We feel ill at ease in the presence of the manager.

EASY

Take the easy way out: try to wriggle out of a problem with the least demanding action
She took the easy way out and did not commit herself to the request.

Go easy: work moderately
She should go easy on her work schedule as she is expecting a baby.

Stand easy: stand relaxed or comfortably
They stood easy when the chief guest addressed the gathering.

EAT

Eat like a horse: glutton
If he eats like a horse all the time, how will he lose weight?

Eat one's heart out: depressed or pining
He is eating his heart out since the day the girl ditched him.

Eat one's words: go back on one's words
After getting the property in his name he is eating his words and behaving awkwardly.

EBB

The ebb and flow: increase and decrease
The ebb and flow of tide kept the ship at bay.

On the ebb: reducing or declining
As we age our will power is also on the ebb.

EFFECT

Bring something into effect: implement or achieve results.
The rule of wearing helmets will be brought into effect from April 1st.

Take effect: produce results
The medicine is now taking effect on his health and we can see the improvement.

To this /that effect: with this / that meaning or information
She sent a message to the effect that she would not be attending the general body meeting.

EGGS

Put all eggs in one basket: risk everything you have on one venture
By putting all the eggs in one basket he stands to lose a lot of money.

A bad egg: a useless person
He is a bad egg and it is better to exclude him from the team.

Have an egg on one's face: feel stupid or foolish
When we went to the party, we had eggs on our faces as it was a theme party and we were not prepared for it.

ELBOW

Out at the elbows: old and full of holes
He insists on wearing that coat, though it is out at the elbows.

EIGHT

Have had one over the eight: slightly drunk
He walked into the office this morning looking like he had had one over the eight.

EMBARRASSMENT

An embarrassment of riches: too many good things to choose from
She has an embarrassment of riches, so she has no problem to adjust.

Get hold of the wrong end of the stick: misinterpret or misunderstand a situation
When he talks it is very easy to get hold of the wrong end of the stick.

END

Be at an end: final stage
The movie was at an end when the power went off.

At the end of the day: when all the pros and cons are weighed equally
At the end of the day there was no point in continuing the relationship when there were so many differences.

In the end: at last, finally
In the end, the agreement was made.

Put an end to one's life: kill oneself
Unable to bear the torture she put an end to her life.

Not the end of the world: things can be worse
He failed in the examinations, but it is not the end of the world. He can try again.

Make both ends meet: try to meet one's expenses
With both their salaries they found it difficult to make both ends meet.

EVEN

Get even with: take revenge
She was determined to get even with her boyfriend for cheating on her.

Even as: just as or exactly when
Even as I was getting ready for the party my friends called me to hurry up.

Even if: in spite of
Even if I want to walk ten miles I want to see the show.

An even chance of doing something: unequally balanced chance or probability
It looks like she has an even chance of winning this election.

EVENT

In any event: anyhow
In any event she cannot win the race with her injury.

In the event of: occurrence of something
In the event of an accident, there is a replacement ready to join the team.

EVER

As bad as ever: the same degree as before
Though the arrangement was good the behaviour of the public was as bad as ever.

Ever more: continually, endlessly
Her fame as a good administrator grew ever more with each passing day.

Ever since: continuously since
Ever since she cut her hair she looks more sophisticated.

For ever and ever: always
I will be your friend for ever and ever.

EVIDENCE

Be in evidence: clearly or easily spotted
They make a good pair and are in evidence at any gatherings

EXAMPLE

For example: for instance
There are so many colours to choose from for that dress, for example, red or orange.

Set an example: behave in a way worthy or unworthy of imitation
She set an example to her juniors by becoming a very hard working student.

EXCEPTION

Make an exception: be partial to someone as a special case
All the students had to submit the assignment but in her case the teacher made an exception.

EXHIBITION

Make an exhibition of oneself: act stupidly or badly in public places
She made an exhibition of herself at the party last evening by drinking and talking too much.

EXPENSE

At one's expense: at the cost of
We ate at the restaurant at the expense of the company.

At the expense of something: with loss or damage to something
She bought a piece of jewellery at the expense of her husband's hard-earned money.

EYE

Set eyes on something: catch sight of something
While window shopping, I set my eyes on the beautiful watch.

For somebody's eyes only: for the person concerned only
The gift is for the bride's eyes only.

Have eyes in the back of one's head: keenly observe
He has eyes in the back of his head and is always alert.

Under one's very eyes: under one's presence
The accident happened under my very eyes.

Eye of the wind: point from which the wind is blowing
The trekkers were facing the eye of the wind.

Have eyes bigger than the stomach: eat more than you can, or be greedy
The glutton has eyes bigger than his stomach.

Keep one's eyes peeled: be very observant
He was keeping his eyes peeled for the beautiful girl.

See something with half an eye: just a passing glance
She noticed the man with half an eye and decided to ignore him.

F

FACE

Face to face: in front of each other.
It was a very good experience coming face to face with the sage.

Have the face to: impertinence, or boldness
He had the face to call on us after having put us into so much trouble.

Put on a bold face: seemingly a brave appearance
He put a bold face and went to attend the marriage of his ex-girlfriend.

Let's face it: we must accept
Let's face it, we have to attend the meeting whether we like it or not.

FACT

Facts and figures: correct data
In order to make a decision we need all the facts and figures.

In fact: truthfully
In fact, you are even allowed to stand on top of that building.

FAIR

A fair question: open-minded or unbiased question
"The girl is smart and qualified, then why is her application rejected?"
"That is a fair question."

Fair enough: acceptable
Fair enough, let's meet half way through.

Fair weather friend: one who is a friend as long as it is advantageous
All fair weather friends desert you once they know you are of no use to them.

Fair and square: right on target
He hit the target fair and square in the middle.

FALSE

A false alarm: a hoax warning
The news about the cyclone to the fishermen was a false alarm.

False move: erroneous action
One false move in the trail and we stand to lose the case.

Under false pretence: wrongly fabricated move
He got the sanctions under false pretences.

FAR

As far as: a great deal
As far as I can see there is no future in this relationship.

By far: a long way
By far this is the longest road that I have travelled.

Carry something too far: carry something beyond a certain limit
They believe in carrying their enmity too far.

Far and wide: everywhere
The fame of the store spread far and wide.

Far from it: certainly not
If you think she is helping me, it is far from it—she has a motive to it.

Go far: climb the ladder of success
As a musician he will go far in this country.

FAST

Fast and furious: energetic and lively
We spent a fast and furious evening at the discotheque.

Play fast and loose with someone: be unsure of one's feelings and flirt around
It is high time he stopped playing fast and loose and settles down with one girl.

FAT

The fat is in the fire: troubled situation becoming even worse
If his father hears that he has failed in his exams again, there will be fat in the fire.

FATE

A fate worse than death: a very bad experience
Recovering from that car accident was a fate worse than death.

FAULT

At fault: responsible for a mistake
The driver was at fault and this caused the accident.

FAVOUR

In favour of somebody/something: support of or payable to in case of cheques
He is in favour of the democrats.

The cheques should be in favour of the company.

FEAR

For the fear of something: apprehensive about
We have to move very carefully for the fear of waking up the children.

In fear of one's life: have a phobia about one's safety
The convict escaped and the people of the town were in fear of their lives.

FEEL

Feel as if: have a hunch
I feel as if I will never wake up tomorrow.

Feel it in one's bones that: have an intuition
I feel it in my bones that we will win the match today.

Feel like doing something: urge to do something
I feel like having dinner out today.

Feel free: grant permission
Feel free to borrow any book from my collection.

FEELERS

Put out feelers: try to get reactions or feedback
We put out feelers to the public asking their opinion about the launch of our new product.

FEW

Few and far between: not too often , with long durations
The shots in the distance were few and far between.

FIDDLE

Be on the fiddle: be corrupt or be a fraud
He was on the fiddle at the time of signing the contract.

To play second fiddle: be a subordinate
He loves to play second fiddle to the manager in the office.

FIGHT

Fight like a tiger: attack someone or defend oneself
He had to fight like a tiger to get what was due to him.

Fight to the finish: struggle till you win
In the family feud she fought to the finish before she won the lawsuit.

FILL

Fill somebody's shoes: stand in for someone or represent another person in their absence
He filled in his father's shoes at the general body meeting very efficiently.

FILTHY

Filthy lucre: monetary gain
He was ready to do anything for filthy lucre.

FIND

Find fault: detect the mistake
The manager has to find fault with all our work.

Find oneself: discover oneself
After I read that spiritual book I found myself.

Find one's way: learn the correct route
With the landmark we have provided they will be able to find their way here.

FINGERS

Pull one's finger out: quit being lazy and get to work
Pull a finger out and complete the project before the manager arrives.

Have a finger in every pie: get involved in everything that is happening
She has a finger in every pie of the festivities.

Lay a finger on someone or something: touch

You lay a finger on that girl and I will take care of you.

Put one's finger on something: discover the cause of the problem
Finally I am able to put my fingers on the problem—I am very slow at work.

Have one's finger on the pulse: keep updated about the latest developments
Though he was old, he had his finger on the pulse of the younger generation.

FIRE

Hold one's fire: cease fire
The army made a pact with the defaulters and decided to hold fire for a month.

On fire: burning or raging passion or fury
The factory building was on fire

When he saw her success his stomach was on fire.

Under fire: criticised or blamed
The whole unit came under fire from the CEO for lack of unity.

Play with fire: risk something dangerous
Getting involved with him is like playing with fire.

Fire and sword: killings in war
The fire and sword at the recent wars have had a bad influence on the society.

Set the Thames on fire: an outstanding achievement
She is sure to set the Thames on fire with her latest novel.

Get through fire and water: endure danger for the sake of others
He was ready to get through fire and water to win his boss's trust.

FIRST

At first: in the beginning
At first I did not like being her friend.

First of all: most importantly
First of all, please find yourselves a place to sit and eat.

First and foremost: before anything else
First and foremost I would like to introduce you to my family.

FISH

Neither fish nor fowl: something not fitting in any category
Her collection of clothes is neither fish nor fowl and is not suitable for this occasion.

A queer fish: a person with weird habits
He is such a queer fish that he does not get along with anyone.

Have other fish to fry: have other errands or things to do
I have other fish to fry than sit to here and wait for him.

FIT

Fit as a fiddle: very healthy
At the age of eight she is fit as a fiddle

Think fit to do something: presume it right to do something
We thought it fit to find a suitable groom for her when she returned from abroad.

Throw a fit: react shockingly
She threw a fit when she found he had cheated on her.

FLASH

Flash in the pan: a quick or brief success that might not repeat again
Like a flash in the pan we won the championship this year as we got a walkover from the opponents.

FLAT

Flat as a pancake: completely levelled
The ground is as flat as a pancake.

Fall flat on one's face: face a setback
The project was unsuccessful and the whole team of engineers had a fall on their face.

Flat out: at full speed, all out
I was flat out after that bumpy journey in the jeep.

FLESH

Flesh and blood: human body
Everyone was shocked to see him in flesh and blood when they had thought he was dead.

One's own flesh and blood: one's own relatives
His own flesh and blood cheated him out of his property.

FLUTTER

Flutter the dovecotes: frighten or alarm people
He fluttered the dovecotes with startling revelations.

FLY

Fly high: be ambitious
With the present position it is possible for her to fly high.

Fly into a rage: flare with anger
When the boss came to know of his absence at the meeting he flew into a rage.

Make sparks fly: cause trouble
At the group discussion the sparks flew while discussing a sensitive topic.

Not hurt a fly: be very soft and gentle-hearted person
She is so soft she won't hurt a fly.

Fly in the ointment: a small hitch in a happy event
We were having a great time at the party, when the only fly in the ointment was the drunken brawl.

FOLLOW

Follow one's example: learn from others
We must try and follow the example he has set for us to become successful .

Follow suit: act in the same manner as someone.
The cap seller threw down the cap from his head and the monkeys followed suit.

FOOD

Food for thought: give some serious thought
Her strange behaviour is certainly food for thought.

FOOL

A fool's paradise: superficial happiness that is short lived
She is living in a fool's paradise that the riches are all hers.

Make a fool of oneself: act foolishly or become a laughing stock
By coming to the party uninvited, she made a fool of herself.

Be a fool for one's pains; a thankless effort
We were fools for our pains to host the guests in our house.

FOOT/FEET

Be on one's feet: keep standing
At the carnival stall we had to be on our feet the whole day.

Have one foot in the grave: terminally ill or have little time to live
She is ninety years old and has one foot in the grave.

Ten feet tall: proud of one's achievements
She felt ten feet tall when she topped the class in the exams this year.

On foot: walking
We covered the entire locality on foot to campaign for the leader.

Put one's feet up: rest or relax
After a tiring day at the office, I just want to put my feet up and rest.

Set foot in: enter
As soon as she set foot in the classroom there was silence.

Put one's foot down: deny or prohibit
When he tried to misbehave with her, she put her foot down and dealt with him.

Put one's foot in: utter something stupid or foolish
I put my foot in it when I asked Jim about his divorced wife.

FORELOCK

Touch, tug one's forelock: touch one's forehead as a mark of respect
When the major died, the whole army touched their forelock as a mark of respect.

FORM

Good form: acceptable standard
She is always in good form when it comes to handling the elderly people.

Form of address: way of addressing someone in speech or writing
The form of address should always be given prime importance in any speech.

Out of form: performance below expectancy
The way he played today's match goes to show that he is out of form.

FORTUNE

Fortunes of war: good or bad effects of war
There was mass destruction of properties due to the fortunes of war.

FOUL

Foul one's own nest: disgrace one's own family
She fouled her own nest by cheating on her husband

FRAME

A frame of mind: mood or state of mind
After the accident he is not in a clear frame of mind.

A frame of reference: set of rules or principles to pass judgementup
We were able to finish the project with the frame of reference our professor had drawn up for us.

FREE

Get/have a free hand: decisions or actions according to one's own will

He was given a free hand to host the programmes for television.

Of one's own free will: according to one's wish

She came to attend the wedding of her own free will.

FROG

A frog in one's throat: a temporary gruffness or hoarse voice

When I went up on stage to face the audience I had a frog in my throat.

FRY

Out of the frying pan into the fire: go into a worse situation from a bad one

He went out of the frying pan into the fire when he divorced his first wife and married the young girl who cheated him.

FULL

Come full circle: return to the same point after going round different events

Her life has come full circle now that she has money to spend.

At full blast: at maximum power or activity

The party was going on full blast when we entered at midnight.

Full of life: energetic or active

Little children are full of life and they bring immense joy.

Full of oneself: boastful or selfish

He is so full of himself that he fails to see the problems of others.

In full: completely

We have cleared our loans in full to the bank.

To the full: to the last capacity

We have to fill the juice to the full in order to serve all the people in the room.

FUND

In funds: having money to spend

Since the company is now in funds, it can employ more people.

FUNERAL

That's my funeral: that's my unpleasant responsibility
"Work hard, or you'll fail." "That is my funeral, not yours."

FUNNY

Funny business: something that is not approved of; illegal
I want none of your funny business.

G

GAIN

Gain ground: advancement or progress
The movement against child labour is gaining ground in our city.

Gain time: obtain extra time by making excuses
To finish the project we had to give the professor a lot of excuses and gain sufficient time.

GAME

Play according to the rules: adhere to the rules of the game or play fair
He believes in playing the game according to the rules.

The name of the game: motto of the organisation
The name of the game in your firm is to put the customer before anything else.

The game is up: when the plan is spoiled
She knew her game was up when she was caught red-handed.

The game is not worth the candle: wasted efforts for a little gain
The game is not worth the candle when we stand to gain very little from it.

Give the game away: leak out a secret
She gave the game away by telling the family about our plans.

The name of the game: the main characteristics
The name of the game in our firm is to please the customer.

GARDEN

Lead someone up the garden path: mislead someone
He led us up the garden path by giving us wrong directions.

GAUNTLET

Take up the gauntlet: accept the challenge
They decided to take up the gauntlet and play another match.

Run the gauntlet: be a party to criticism or blame
Being at the topmost position in an organisation, you have to run the gauntlet of your subordinates.

GENERAL

As a general rule: customary
As a general rule women are not admitted to this course.

In general: commonly or mostly
In general all the children in the class are above average.

GETTING

Can't get over something: can't recover from
She still can't get over the debacle of the project.

Get away from it all: break free from usual routine
I had enough of tension and decided to get away from it all and attend a meditation camp.

There's no getting away from something: there is no escape
There is no getting away from family problems, we have to face it.

GHOST

Ghost town: uninhabited town
After the earthquake the city of Bhuj was a ghost town.

Give up the ghost: stop making an effort
When he failed in the exams he gave up the ghost without trying for the second time.

GIFT

A gift from the gods: unexpected success
It was a gift from the gods when there was a downpour during summer.

The gift of the gab: the ability to dominate a conversation
He is definitely fit for marketing as he has the gift of the gab.

Look a gift horse in the mouth: refuse or ridicule a token of gift got for nothing
She looked a gift horse in the mouth showing her foolishness.

GILD

Gild the lily: enhance or brighten up
He had to gild the lily before making the presentation to his boss.

Gild the truth: disguise or camouflage
She had to gild the truth about her identity to the shopkeeper.

GIRD

Gird up one's loins: prepare for battle, or get ready
The army decided to gird up its loins and start moving towards the border.

GLAD

Glad rags: best attire
At the launch party it was nice to see her in her glad rags.

Somebody's goods and chattels: personal belongings
He decided to run away from his house with all his goods and chattels.

GLANCE

At a glance: with one fleeting look
She was able to judge the mood of the class with one glance at the students.

At first glance: look for the first time
At the first glance it seemed easy.

GO

Anything goes: anything is acceptable
After her success anything she says goes in the office.

Go all out: put in best efforts
We have to go all out to get the firm order.

Go on: continue
He cannot go on with this rude behaviour in the office.

At one go: all together.
The successful projects of the year demanded for a celebration all at one go.

GOD

God willing: favourably
God willing, she must be able to score high marks in the exams.

In God's name: used to ask and explanation in anger or surprise
What in God's name is he doing here at this hour?

GOOD

A good few: used to denote the number of people
A good few people came to listen to the lecture.

For good: permanently
She is leaving her husband for good.

As good as: almost
This old cot is as good as new.

Do one good: benefit a person
It will do you good to take those extra lessons.

GORGE

Make somebody's gorge rise: anger someone
The sight of the kidnapper made her gorge rise.

GRACE

Have the grace to do something: be polite enough to do something
He should have the grace to thank all the people who stood by him at the difficult times.

With good grace: willingly
She acknowledged the gifts with good grace and sent thank-you cards.

A saving grace: being bailed out of a situation
The only saving grace of the function was good food.

GRASP

Grasp the nettle: deal with a situation in an efficient and bold manner
When the business was under loss, he grasped the nettle and emerged a winner.

GRASS

Put somebody out of grass: force one to retirement due to old age
She was put to grass though she was hale and hearty.

Not let the grass grow under one's feet: not waste time in executing a task given
He is not a person to let grass the grow under his feet when so much has to be done with the firm.

GREAT

Going great guns: doing excellently
The training to the students is going great guns for the project.

Great and small: everything powerful or weak/everyone rich or poor.
Great and small attended the prince's wedding.

GRIM

Like grim death: adamant or unyielding
She stuck to her decision like grim death and was ready to face the consequences.

GRIN

Grin and bear: put up with
He had to grin and bear his grief at the function.

GRIND

Grind the faces of the poor: cause suffering to the poor and needy
The rich landlord ground the faces of the poor and destroyed the huts and belongings of the slum dwellers.

Grind on: continue something for a long time
The chief guest ground on his speech in spite of the bored look on the faces of the audience.

GRIP

Get a grip on oneself: control oneself
During the fight she got a grip on herself and offered to mediate.
Come to grips with: find a solution to a problem
She had to come to grips with her sorrow and look after her children.

GROUND

Fresh ground: new method
They had to fight the case on fresh ground.
Gain ground: make progress
She is gaining ground in the new project.
Prepare the ground: establish a base
His research helped prepare the ground for further inventions.
To the ground: demolish fully
The town was razed to the ground after the bomb blast.

GUM

Gum up the works: stop the machines or systems
They gummed up the whole works by trying out this new machine.

GUARD

On one's guard: being careful
We have to be on our guard when we are travelling alone.
Stand guard: protect
Till the family came he had to stand guard over the broken door.

H

HABIT

Get into the habit of: addiction, fixation

She had got into the habit of chain smoking.

Make a habit of: inclination or tendency

She made a habit of checking every file that came to her table.

HACKLES

Make someone's hackles rise: anger someone

She made the old man's hackles rise by nagging him about his age.

With one's hackles up: angered and ready to fight

With his hackles up, he was waiting to strike the enemy with all his might.

HAIR

Keep your hair on: keep calm

Keep your hair on—do not let a rogue like him disturb you.

Make one's hair curl: scare or frighten one

The horror movie made our hair curl.

Not turn a hair: not showing any reaction or emotion

They did not turn a hair when she narrated the story of the gruesome murder.

HALF

Go half and half: share equally

We decided to share the hotel bill half and half.

Half a second: in a short time
She will be here in half a second.

HAND

By hand: manual
This embroidery is made by hand, so it is expensive.

From hand to hand: pass on from person to person
The files were passed on from hand to hand before it finally reached the manager.

Win somebody's hand: make somebody promise to marry one
The princess won the charming prince's hand.

Hand in glove: linked or associated
The politicians are hand in glove with the terrorists.

Hand in hand: linking each other's hands
The children crossed the road hand in hand.

Hands off: don't touch
He has decided to lay his hands off the project.

In hand: under control
The matter is in hand with the manager.

Try one's hand: make an attempt
These holidays I decided to try my hand at painting.

Have one's hand full: be very busy
She had her hands full looking after the four children.

Live from hand to mouth: bare existence
After he lost the job the family had to live a hand to mouth existence.

All hands to the pump: everyone to lend a helping hand
The project must be submitted by tomorrow so all hands to the pump!

Not do a hand's turn: not work
You cannot expect promotions when you do not do a hand's turn at the office.

Off one's hand: not one's responsibility anymore
I cannot take any decisions as this project is off my hands now.

Throw one's hand in: give up or abandon a job one is doing
As this experiment is not yielding any result it is better he throws his hand in and move on to another one.

HANDY

Come in handy: be useful
Her language skills will come in handy to clinch the deal.

HANG

Hang in balance: a point where the decision may go either way
The decision of the sale is hanging in balance for want of permission from the ministry.

Get the hang: grasp the details
I am yet to get a hang of the new syllabus.

HARD

Hard as nails: tough-hearted or unsympathetic
The old woman will not part with anything—she is hard as nails.

Hard as stone: firm or unshakable
The chapattis at the restaurant are hard as stones.

Hard luck: misfortune
It is hard luck that he failed in the examination

Hard of hearing: deaf
You have to talk very loudly as I am hard of hearing.

The hard way: tough way or difficult method
I learnt the hard way to deal with disappointments.

No hard feelings: no ill feelings, or bitterness
Though they broke off all relationships there were no hard feelings.

Hard up for something: insufficient
She is so hard up for money that she had to sell all her gold.

Hard and fast: very rigid
The rules of the military are hard and fast.

Make hard work of something: make something seem it is more difficult than it is.
She always makes a hard work of her cooking.

Take a hard line over something: adamant about a decision
She took a hard line over the decision about not attending her sister's wedding.

HARE

Run with the hare and hunt with the hounds: be friendly with both sides in a dispute

It is always wise to run with the hare and hunt with the hounds in a family dispute.

HASTE

In haste: in a hurry
The house was sold in haste.

Make haste: be quick
Make haste or we will miss the beginning of the movie.

HAUL

Haul somebody over the coals: scold or reprove someone
The children were hauled over the coals for not behaving well.

HAVE

Have had it: no chance of success or no hope
He won't win now, he's had it.

Have got to: must or obligation
I have got to attend the marriage of my boss this evening.

HAWK

Know a hawk from a handsaw: being able to judge fairly
I can tell a hawk from a handsaw when I meet one.

HAY

Make hay of someone or something: cause confusion
They made hay of my presentation at the seminar.

HEAD

From head to foot: from top to bottom
The children were covered with mud from head to foot.

Go to one's head: become proud
The recognition has gone to his head.

Head over heels: completely
He was head over heels in love with the girl at first sight.

In one's head: rooted in memory
It is difficult for the children to keep so many facts in their heads.

Keep one's head: be calm or composed
Even during the financial crisis he kept his head.

Above one's head: unable to comprehend

The new science syllabus is way above my head.

Get it into one's head: understand
Please get it into your head that you have to be punctual to the office.

Heads will roll: concerned persons will be pulled up for questioning
If the financial scam comes out in the open many heads will roll.

HEART

At heart: trait or nature
He is a gem of a person at heart.

From the heart: sincerely
I send my good wishes from the heart.

Have a heart: please be kind / merciful
Have a heart—he is still a small boy.

A heart of gold: good-natured person
Though he looks tough he has a heart of gold.

To one's heart's content: to the satisfaction of
After my tooth was pulled out I ate ice-creams to my heart's content.

A heart of stone: hard-hearted
She will never forget or forgive for she has a heart of stone.

Take something to heart: be depressed
She has taken the accident to heart and is not being cooperative.

With one's heart in one's mouth: with fear and worry
When we sat on the big giant wheel I had my heart in my mouth.

HEEL

At the heel of someone/something: follow closely
We were at the heels of the bus which showed us the way to the village.

Under the heel of somebody: being dominated by someone
She is always under the heel of her mother-in-law and cannot think independently.

HELL

All hell broke loose: confusion
When the banks suddenly went on strike all hell broke loose.

Give someone hell: give a hard time / rebuke someone
She gave him hell for cheating on her.

Hell for leather: as fast as possible
We ran hell for leather when it started raining heavily last evening.

Come hell or high waters: whatever the obstruction is
Come hell or high waters we have to reach the place before dusk.

HELP

Help a lame dog over a stile: help someone in trouble
He believed in helping a lame dog over a stile throughout his life.

HERE

Here and there: in different places
We can find water here and there.

Here below: under the earth
We have a gold mine right here below.

HIDE

Hide one's light under a bushel: be modest about one's talents or achievements
Do not hide your light under a bushel—let the world know how talented you are!

Neither hide nor hair of someone/something: without trace
We could find neither hide nor hair of the robbers after they ran away with the loot.

HIGH

Get on one's high horse: act haughty
Once he became rich he got on his high horse and ignored everyone.

High and dry: stranded or ignored
He was left high and dry at the party last evening.

High and mighty: arrogant
Due to his high connection he is always acting high and mighty.

High days and holidays: special occasions or festivals
They visit us on all high days and holidays.

In high dudgeon: furious and resentful
He walked out of the meeting in high dudgeon.

Stink to high heaven: have a bad or unpleasant odour.
The rotten mangoes were stinking to high heaven in the kitchen counter.

Be for a high jump: likely to be punished severely
You'll be for the high jump when the teacher knows you have not completed the assignment.

HILL

A hill of beans: something that has very little value
The coat she wore for the wedding is worth a hill of beans.

HIT

Hit the bottle: get drunk often
It is his habit to hit the bottle every night.

Hit it off: take to each other; get on good terms
We hit it off at the first meeting itself.

Hit the jackpot: become rich instantly
We hit the jackpot when our names were selected for the prize.

Hit the road: start a journey
We hit the road at the break of dawn.

HOLE

Hole in the wall: a small or tiny café, room or shop in between a building
Though his shop is a hole in the wall, it does very good business.

HOLLOW

Have hollow legs: have a big appetite
It is very common for teenagers to have hollow legs.

Come home to roost: come back to cause problems
The disobedient boy is coming home to roost.

HOME

At home: feel comfortable
We made ourselves at home until she returned from work.

A home bird: prefers to stay indoors
He is a home bird and hates to go outdoors on weekends.

HONOUR

Do the honours: conduct the proceedings
Please do the honours of proposing the vote of thanks.

Have the honour of: be privileged to
Let me have the honour of escorting you to the party.

In honour of somebody: out of respect for somebody
The meeting was held in honour of his achievements.

HOOK

Let off the hook: out of trouble or difficulty
She was winning but then let her opponent off the hook.

Be hooked on someone: be attracted to or infatuated with
He was hooked on to the girl next door.

Get hooked on something: addicted to
He got hooked on to drugs and had to go for rehabilitation.

HOPE

Beyond hope: no remedy
It was beyond hope to expect him to recover after that accident.

Raise somebody's hope: encourage somebody to expect better fortune
When the sun came out late in the afternoon, it raised our hope of attending the function.

Shatter somebody's hopes: discourage someone
She shattered my hopes of getting admission when she told me that the last date was over.

The in hope that: wishful that
We waited for a four hours in the hope that we could meet the manager.

Hope for the best: wish for the best
We must always hope for the best and put in our sincere efforts.

HORN

On the horns of a dilemma: choosing between two equally desired things
I was on the horns of a dilemma when I had to choose between my children and husband.

HORSE

Change horses in midstream: jump from one errand to another leaving one unfinished.
If you have started this story first it is better to finish than change horses in midstream.

HOT

The hot seat: high position
To reach the hot seat politicians will do anything.

Hot spot: areas prone to trouble
The railway station is the hot spot of the city.

HOUR

After hours: after the specified time
She always held meetings with the staff after hours.

At the eleventh hour: last minute
We had to prepare the project report at the eleventh hour.

HOUSE

On the house: complimentary or free of charge
At the resort all our meals were on the house.

Bring the house down: capture the whole-hearted attention of the audience
The dancers brought the house down with their stunning performance.

Get on like house on fire: compatibility or getting along very well with someone
When we realised that we had the same thoughts we got along like a house on fire.

HUFF

Huff and puff: show anger
She huffed and puffed when she found that the papers were misplaced.

HURRY

In a hurry: impatient
She is always in a hurry to do all her chores.

In no hurry: not eager to
He is in no hurry to finish the assignment on time.

I

ICE

On ice: kept cold
The beer bottles were kept on ice before the party.

Break the ice: start the conversation
At any gathering he is the one to break the ice and mix freely.

Cut no ice: have any effect
His boastings will cut no ice with the audience.

IDEA

Get the idea: perception or understanding
Get the idea that this mission is impossible.

Give somebody ideas: give false encouragement
Don't give her false ideas that entering the beauty pugent is beneficial.

Have no idea: have no clue
I have no idea where to look for the file.

IF

If and when: possibility of any event.
If and when I become rich I will buy this big mansion.

If only: used to express a wish
If only I was tall I could take part in that play.

ILL

Ill at ease: not comfortable
In the company of boys she is always ill at ease.

An ill wind: a bad phase/time
The recent happenings is the effect of an ill wind and is bound to change soon.

IMPULSE

On impulse: on the spur of the moment; sudden desire
On an impulse we decided to go on a picnic.

IN

Be in for something: about to experience something
When the teacher comes the children are in for a thrashing.

In and out: inside and outside
The dog kept running in and out of the house to show his happiness.

INCH

By inches: very little
The traffic on the road was moving by inches.

Every inch: fully; completely
We went through every inch of the room but did not find the gold ring.

Inch by inch: little by little
The army was able to scale the mountain inch by inch.

INNINGS

Have had a good innings: have had a long and successful life
He must not complain anymore, since he has had a long innings in his life.

INSULT

Insult to somebody's intelligence: errand or excuse too silly or foolish to be given importance
Believing in her honesty is an insult to my intelligence.

INTENT

To all intents and purposes: in practical terms, virtually
To all intents and purposes this theory is useless but is still included in the syllabus.

INTEREST

In somebody's interest: to the advantage of somebody
In the best interest of her daughter she must quit her job.

IRON

Have many irons in the fire: have many interests or many resources
He has many irons in the textile business.

ITCH

Have an itching palm: have a greed for wealth and money
He was doomed as he had an itching palm.

Have an itchy feet: have an urge to travel or move about restlessly
She has an itchy feet and it is difficult to tie her down.

ITSELF

By itself: automatically
The membership will get cancelled by itself if we do not pay the dues.

IVORY

An ivory tower: live a life cocooned away from realities and hardship
Living in your ivory tower, you don't know about the life in a village.

J

JAW

One's jaw drops: amazed or surprised
His jaw dropped when she proposed to him.

JEST

In jest: in fun
His reply was taken half in jest.

JOB

A good job: good work
You have done a good job of raising your son.

On the job: while working
He continued his studies while on the job itself.

Out of job: unemployed
Due to the factory lock up many workers were out of job for one year.

JOIN

Join the club: similar events happening to many people at the same time.
I heard that you have also been made a victim of April Fools' Day—join the club!

Join forces: partner someone to achieve a particular goal
Like-minded people of the building joined forces to fight for their rights.

Join hands: hold hands or come together

Let us join hands and pray for the departed soul.

JOKE

Make a joke on somebody/something: make fun of somebody or something
The children always made a joke of the teacher who had a funny accent.

Play a joke: play a prank or trick
The boys decided to play a joke on the newcomers.

JUMP

Jump for joy: leap with delight
She jumped with joy when she found that she topped her class in the exams.

Jump the gun: act before it is necessary
Do not jump the gun and meet the advocate.

Jump out of one's skin: show surprise
The loud music at the cinema hall made us jump out of our skins.

Jump to conclusions: take a decision before weighing the pros and cons.
Do not jump to conclusions regarding the status of the company.

Keep one jump ahead of someone: be one step ahead of someone
We have to keep one jump ahead of our children to understand them better.

Jump bail: fail to appear in court after being released on bail
Once the businessman was out of prison, he decided to jump bail and escape.

JUST

Just about: barely enough
I had just bout enough money for my train fare.

Just any: whichever
Before choosing just any dress we want, we have to check the price .

Just in case: precaution
Just in case the baby wakes up please let me know.

Just like that: without any warning
The principal walked into the classroom just like that.

Just now: the very moment
I need to reach home just now.

JUSTICE

Bring someone to justice: arrest, try and sentence a criminal
The honest judge was able to bring justice in the long pending case.

Do justice to something/someone: be fair
Do justice to your parents and find yourself a good profession.

JUGULAR

Go for the jugular: attack the weak point of the opponent
Go for the jugular and try to win this match for us!

K

KEEP

Keep it up: maintain the good job
You have won the trophy again this year—keep it up!

For keeps: permanently
I will never let you down, for this relationship is for keeps.

KICK

Kick up a fuss: cause confusion
She kicked up a fuss regarding her place in the bus.

Kick the bucket: die
The old man kicked the bucket.

KILL

Kill onself: overwork
To earn more money he killed himself.

Kill or cure: succeed or fail miserably
The new project can be a real kill or a cure.

Kill time: spend time idly
When the teacher did not come to class the children started playing a game to kill time.

KIND

In kind: articles or things and not money
For a wedding gift cash is better than kind.

Kind of: a bit
He felt kind of shy to ask for a loan.

KNIFE

Get one's knife into somebody: try to cause harm
The manager was so angry with the peon for stealing that he could get a knife into him.

Like a knife through butter: without difficulty, smoothly
He ran the race ahead of everyone else from the start like a knife through butter.

KNOCK

Knock it off: stop the noise
Knock it off, girls, the chief guest is here to talk to you.

Knock someone sideways: stun someone
He knocked me sideways when he offered to help me with the cleaning.

KNOW

Be known to somebody: be familiar to someone
She better watch out her reputation, she is well known to the public.

Know all the answers: be very well informed or articulate
She will be the right candidate for the elections as she knows all the answers.

Know something backwards: be thorough
The child knows the letters of the alphabet backwards.

Know someone by sight: recognise or recall someone's face without actually knowing them well
He is my husband's friend, but I know him only by sight.

Know best: be the best judge
The teacher knows best when he appoints the prefect.

Knows one's way around: be familiar with the routes/ place
I don't need any directions as I know my way around the city.

Knows no bounds: limitless
My love for you knows no bounds.

Let somebody know: inform
When we reach the destination we will let you know.

You never know: you cannot be sure
You never know, this change may do him good.

KEEN

Keen as mustard: very eager
She is keen as a mustard to finish the project and submit it tomorrow.

KEEP

Keep up with the Joneses: try to maintain the status as one's neighbour
Trying to keep up with the Joneses is a foolish thing to do.

KICK

Kick against the pricks: hurt oneself by useless resistance
The prisoner kicked against the pricks while trying to free himself.

Kick over the traces: refuse to accept control or discipline
Children these days kick over the traces and misbehave most of the time.

KILL

Kill with kindness: be excessively kind
The old lady will kill you with excessive kindness when you visit her.

KING

A king's ransom: large sum of money
The bunglow cost him a king's ransom.

KINGDOM

Till kingdom come: forever
I will wait for you till kingdom come.

KNICKERS

Get one's knickers in a twist: be confused or disoriented
This is not a serious problem and there is no need to get your knickers in a twist.

KITCHEN

Everything but the kitchen sink: every movable object
The robbers looted everything but the kitchen sink.

KITTENS

Have kittens: be tensed or worried
He was having kittens till the order was finalised by the authorities.

KNOCK

Knock the stuffing out of : demoralise or weaken someone
The surgery has knocked the stuffing out of him.

Knock them in the aisles: get the audience's approval
His brilliant performance on stage this evening knocked them in the aisles.

KNUCKLE

Near the knuckle: nearly indecent to be approved
Her sense of dressing is too near the knuckle for my taste.

KYBOSH

Put the kybosh on someone or something: stop or prevent someone or something
We decided to put the kybosh on his wild ways by getting him married.

L

LABOUR

A labour of Hercules: put immense effort for a certain job
He put on a labour of Hercules to finish the project on time.

A labour of love: job done with great pleasure
This house is their labour of love.

LAND

On the land: working as a farmer
Throughout his life he has toiled on the land.

LAP

In the lap of luxury: richness/wealth
They will not know the meaning of poverty as they have been brought up in the lap of luxury.

LARGE

Large as life: appear in person, seen as live
We saw the actor large as life shooting for a movie in our locality.

By and large: taking everything into account
By and large she is a very lovable person.

Larger than life: huge or exaggerated size
He will be the right candidate for he has a larger than life image with the public.

LAST

Have the last laugh: victory over one's opponents
She had the last laugh when she decided to solve the problem with the help of law.

The last resort: the final hope
In order to save the family we had to go to court as the last resort.

Have the last word: final say in an argument.
The manager refused to listen to any argument and had the last word by adjourning the meeting.

See the last of somebody: not having to see someone again
I hope I see the last of him.

Last but not least: final but not unimportant
Last but not least, I wish you all the very best in your examinations.

LATE

At the latest: not later than
At the latest I need the reports by Monday.

Of late: these days
Of late they have been having a lot of arguments.

Later on: at another time or stage
I will fix up a meeting with the bosses later on.

LATHER

Get into a lather: get angry or upset
He gets into a lather about his employees reporting late for work.

LAUGH

Laugh like a drain: laugh loudly
She laughs like a drain, that does not go with her social status.

Laugh on the other side of one's face: be forced to change from joy to sorrow
The boys laughed on the other side of their faces when they heard that they had failed in the exams.

LAW

Law and order: situation where rules of law are adhered to strictly
The law and order of the country is in the hands of politicians.

Go to law: go to court

When he did not pay up his loans, the firm decided to go to law.

The law of the jungle: survival of the strongest
These days instead of being cordial with each other people follow the law of the jungle.

Lay down the law: lay down the rules/ orders
Before we start functioning as a group we must lay down the laws of the club.

Take the law into one's own hands: decide the action or consequence, not taking law into consideration
He decided to take the law into his own hands when he realised that there was no hope for his family.

LEAST

At least: not less than
At least finish your homework before you go to school tomorrow.

Not in the least: not at all
Her presence is not important at all not in the least.

LEAVE

Leave/let somebody alone: not to be interfered or disturbed
Please leave her alone, for she is very upset.

Leave a bad taste in the mouth: feeling of disgust
The fight between the two brothers left a bad taste in the mouth.

Leave somebody in the lurch: abandon someone in an embarrassing situation
In the middle of the party my escort left me in the lurch and went away home.

Leave it at that: no further arguments
Let us leave it at that and get on with our lives.

Leave no stones unturned: try all possible means
In the matter of the business he never leaves any stone unturned.

LEFT

Have two left feet: be clumsy
He has two left feet and is shy to dance.

Left,right and centre: on all sides
We searched for the book left,right and centre.

LEG

Be all legs: have long limbs and short torso
She is all legs and feels shy to wear short dresses.

Give someone a leg up: support someone
She was given a leg up by all her relatives which made her confident.

LEND

Lend an ear: listen sympathetically
He is such a good friend he lends an ear to all my problems.

Lend a helping hand: assist
By lending a helping hand she makes sure his business is running smoothly.

LENGTH

At length: in great detail
The teacher explained the procedure at length till each of the students understood it.

Go to any lengths: go to any extent
We were prepared to go to any lengths to get the order for the firm.

LETTER

Letter of the law: prescribed form from the words of law
This is a letter of law and needs to be filled up carefully.

LEVEL

Have a level head: controlled thinking
She is a level-headed girl and will not make silly mistakes.

On a level with: equal
She worked hard in her studies until she was on level with her friends.

Level pegging: make progress at the same rate
Both the teams are on a level pegging.

LIBERTY

Liberty hall: space with complete freedom
Her house is a liberty hall which is filled with warmth and happiness.

LIE

Lie in wait: hide
We had to lie in wait for the animals to appear.

Lie heavy on: be a burden
He died with the burden of guilt lying heavily on him.

Lie doggo: lie down still without moving
The thief was lying doggo till he heard the footsteps fade away.

The lie of the land: state of a particular situation
They had to survey the lie of the land before coming to a decision.

LIFE

Come to life: become active or animated
Instead of boring lectures children come to life when taught through stories.

Lay down one's life: give up or sacrifice one's life
Many soldiers lay down their lives everyday protecting our borders.

LIGHT

Bring something to light: reveal or expose
The latest scam has brought to light the involvement of many politicians.

Throw light on something: clarify or clear up
I asked my grandfather to throw light on the age-old dispute of the family.

See the light of day: make a beginning
I don't know when these stories will see the light of day and get published.

As light as a feather: very delicate or light
This saree is as light as a feather and beautiful to drape.

Go out like a light: fall asleep instantly
After a hard day's work I am so tired and go out like a light as soon as I hit the bed.

According to one's light: according to one's belief or ideas
We all react to situations according to our own light.

Stand in somebody's light: stand between a person and the source of light
You'll have to move aside as you are standing in my light.

By the light of nature: without extra guidance or help
By the light of nature he has become very successfully.

LIKELY

Likely story: a doubtful or make-believe story
His is a likely story of how rich and famous he is .

LIMB

Out on a limb: left out or isolated
After her parents died, she was out on a limb .

LIMIT

Off limits: out of bounds
This locality is off limits for a person using the road.

Within limits: hold to some extent
Alcohol should be consumed well within the limits.

LINE

On the same lines: as per specification
The team conducted itself on the same lines taught by the coach.

In the line of duty: during office or performing one's duty
Discipline is a must in any line of duty.

In line with something: along with something
She always keeps in line with the latest fashions and dresses very well.

LIVE

Live within one's means: live according to what you earn
Though she came from a very rich family, she learnt to live within her means after marriage.

Live in hope: look forward to
She lives in hope that he will always come back to her.

Live like a lord: luxurious style of living
Though he is not earning anymore he still lives like a lord.

Live it up: be a spendthrift
Being the only son he is living it up with his father's money.

Live by one's wits: earn with the help of sly and clever means
He believes in living by his wits.

Live on the fat of the land: enjoy best food and drinks
For generations now, they have been living on the fat of the land.

Live off the land: make a living with only agricultural products
After his retirement, the family decided to live off the land they had inherited.

LOAD

Load of dice: put one at a disadvantage

The first time he took part in the competition, he knew he was loaded against all the professionals.

A loaded question: question intended to trap someone
A loaded question from the teacher put all the students out of gear.

LOCK

Under lock and key: safely locked up
The documents of the house are under lock and key.

Lock, stock and barrel: everything a person owns
The whole premises was burgled lock, stock and barrel.

LOCKER

Go to Davy Jones's locker: to the bottom of the sea
All the money he stole went to Davy Jones's locker while he was escaping at sea.

LONG

Go a long way: become very successful
She is very hardworking and clever and will certainly go a long way.

Have come a long way: have made great improvements
From being a small scale industrialist he has come a long way and built an empire.

In the long run: finally
In the long run all his experiences will come of use.

A long shot: guess
Though he was not sure of the answer he took a long shot.

As long as: on condition that
As long as you can digest all the food you can eat as much as you want.

A long haul: long and difficult activity or situation
It has been a long haul but finally we have got adjusted to city life.

LOOSE

At a loose end: free
I decided to go on a spiritual journey as I was at a loose end.

Break loose: free oneself or escape
I have to break loose from this mundane routine someday.

Have a loose tongue: talk too much

He lost his job because of his loose tongue.

LOSE

Lose one's bearings: become confused or irrational
You lose your bearings due to too much strain and stress.

Lose one's breath: pant for breath
The old man lost his breath when he ran after the little child.

Lose courage: depressed or fearful
At times of difficulty we should not lose courage.

Lose face: be humiliated
She lost face when she was verbally attacked for her rude behaviour.

Lose heart: being dejected
The child lost heart when he failed in the examination

Lose sight of: not be able to see
We lost sight of the road as we went deeper into the jungle.

LOT

Fall to somebody's lot: become responsible for something
It fell to my lot to look after her children after her death.

Throw in one's lot with somebody: join up with some to share wealth and fortunes
He decided to throw in his lot with my brother.

LOVE

Fall in love with someone: be attracted to someone
He saw the girl at the wedding and fell in love with her.

For the love of something: passionate about something
For the love of adventure sports we trek every weekend.

LOW

At a low ebb: in a poor state
Her spirits were at a very low ebb.

Be brought low: be reduced in health, wealth or position
Many rich families were brought low by the financial crisis.

Run low: become exhausted
We are running low on petrol.

Lay somebody or something low: weaken or destroy
The whole family was laid low with flu.

LUCK

As luck would have it: fortunately or unfortunately
As luck would have it we were drenched in the rain.

Just one's luck: just one's good or bad fortune
It is just her luck that the holidays have been postponed.

LUNATIC

The lunatic fringe: extreme or eccentric ideals and ways of thinking that is not acceptable normally
They belong to the lunatic fringe and will not get along with anyone.

M

MAD

Like mad: very much
He was in love with her like mad but she did not reciprocate.

MAKE

Make do with something: manage/adjust
Till the rains come the farmers have to make do with the stored water.

Make good: succeed
She made good as a very shrewd housewife.

MALICE

With malice aforethought: having criminal intentions
He decided to join the organization with malice aforethought.

MAN

Every man Jack: every single person
Every man Jack donated for the noble cause.

Be somebody's man: ideal person
If you want good advice on investments he is the man to approach.

Be man enough to do something: be bold and aggressive
Be man enough and own up your faults in the court.

Be one's own man: independent
He is his own man and will never take anyone's help in his personal matters.

The man of the match: best performer in a match

The man of the match was awarded to my brother.

Man to man: one man to another talking openly
They decided to have a man to man discussion about their problems.

MAR

Make or mar: make or break a situation or person
Her decision will make or mar the family fortunes.

MARROW

To the marrow: right through
We felt the warmth to the marrow as soon as we took a sip of the drink.

MARK

Miss the mark: unsuccessful
She missed the mark by an inch and had to pay double the price.

Leave one's mark on something: leave a distinct impression
Though he taught only for one year, he left a mark on every student.

Wide off the mark: irrelevant/inapplicable
His observations were wide off the mark.

Be up to the mark: appropriate
The quality of all the goods sold in this store is up to the mark.

MARKET

Come into the market: be commercially sold
Fake and genuine goods come into the market for sale.

In the market for: interested in selling or buying
He is in the market for buying antique furniture.

MAST

Before the mast: serving as an ordinary seaman
He served for forty years before the mast.

MATTER

As a matter of fact: truthfully
As a matter of fact the crime was not committed by the dead person.

Let the matter rest: not discuss the topic
We decided to let the matter rest and resume our discussion on other topics.

Make matters worse: deteriorate the situation

To make matters worse the couple eloped and got married against the wishes of their parents.

No matter what/who: whatever or whoever
No matter whoever you meet they have the same opinion.

Take matters into one's hand: take a decision by oneself
He took matters into his own hands when he realised that his juniors were not competent enough.

A matter of life and death: seriousness / urgency regarding matters of life
Since it was a matter of life and death the hospital authorities attended to the patient immediately.

Matter of opinion: different views of different people
Whether the decision taken by him is correct or not is a matter of opinion.

MEAL

A square meal: a substantial meal
Half the people in the village do not get a square meal a day.

Make a meal of something: eat more than required
The child made a meal of all the chocolates offered to it.

MEANS

By all means: surely, certainly
You can borrow my books by all means.

By no means: not at all
By no means is this route an easy one to take while trekking.

MEASURE

Beyond measure: greatly / infinitely
Her support for the cause of the poor is beyond measure.

MEAT

Easy meat: easy to defeat
Winning the finals was easy meat to the seasoned players.

MEDICINE

A taste of one's own medicine: return a bad treatment one gives another
She decided to give him a taste of his own medicine by ditching him at the altar.

Take one's medicine: accept an unpleasant situation without complaints
He took his medicine when the authorities raided his premises.

MEET

Meet the case: sufficient
All the clues found meet the case to a great extent.

Meet the eye/ear: be seen or heard
As we neared the stairs loud music met our ears.

Meet someone halfway: come to an understanding or compromise.
If he resigns from the board I am willing to meet you half way and discuss the case.

Meet one's Waterloo: face defeat
At the hands of the junior team they met their Waterloo.

MEMORY

If memory serves: if I remember correctly
If memory serves me right he was limping the last time I saw him.

In memory of somebody: to dedicate in the name of
She dedicated the award in the name of her grandfather who was a great teacher.

MEND

Mend one's ways: change or improve
After she was able to mend her ways she won the trust of his family.

MERCY

At the mercy of somebody: in the control of
The women were at the mercy of the tyrant.

MERRY

Make merry: celebrate, have fun
The children made merry on their picnic to the beach.

METHOD

Method in one's madness: sense in what appears to be foolish or strange
She is behaving very funnily these days but there is a method in her madness.

MIDDLE

Middle of nowhere: isolated

The hut is in the middle of nowhere.

Be somebody's middle name: a person's character or trait
Rudeness is his middle name.

MILLSTONE

A millstone round one's neck: responsibility or accountability
My lies to the children were like a millstone round my neck.

MIND

Spring to mind: come to one's thoughts
An idea sprang to my mind about the various designs available.

Be in two minds about something: doubtful of something
I am two minds about buying that expensive dress.

Take the load of someone's mind: provide relief to a person
His assurance has taken a load of my mind for sometime.

Be out of one's mind: act senselessly
You have to be out of your mind to reject this proposal.

Keep something in mind: remember
Keep in mind while travelling that it is better to travel light.

Have a good mind to do something: urge or desire
I have a good mind to go and have a cup of tea.

Put one's mind to something: concentrate on one thing
Once he puts his mind to something, he never falters.

Turn something over in one's mind: think carefully
After the meeting I turned over in my mind all the matters we discussed before making my decision.

Never mind: don't worry or don't bother
Never mind, we can apply for the course again.

Make up one's mind: decide
I have made up my mind to quit smoking once and for all.

MINE

A mine of information: a storehouse of information
My grandmother is a mine of information regarding family matters.

MINISTER

A ministering angel: person who helps with tenderness

She is a ministering angel when it comes to taking care of children.

MINT

In mint condition: unused or brand new
We sold the car that was in mint condition.

MINUTE

At any minute: very soon
The chief guest will be here in any minute.

Just a minute: wait for a moment
Just a minute, let me think again before I buy that dress.

The minute: as soon as
The minute the gates of the school were opened the children rushed out.

MISS

Something amiss: skip or omit
There is something amiss in theses documents.

Miss the boat: let go of an opportunity
If she does not accept the proposal she will miss the boat to climb up the corporate ladder.

MISTAKE

By mistake: by error or carelessly
By mistake the files were sent to the wrong person.

Make no mistake about something: being misled
He is an honest person but make no mistake, you cannot take him for a ride.

There is no mistaking: there is no possibility of wrong about someone or something
There is no mistaking that her intentions to get close to him are purely for gain.

MIX

Get mixed up in something: become involved in something
We were not ready to get mixed up in her affairs.

Have mixed feelings about someone or something: confused or conflicting feelings
I have mixed feelings about this quotation that we are sending.

MOCKER

Put the mocker on somebody: bring bad luck to somebody
She was always unlucky and put the mockers on her family too.

MONEY

Get one's money's worth: value for money spent
We got our money's worth when we booked our holidays with a tour operator.

Good money: a lot of money
When he sold all his shares he made good money.

Have money to burn: have excess money to spend
He has money to burn so he knows not the value of money.

Make money: profits
We decided to make money with our skills in drawing.

Put money into something: invest
She has put all her money into mutual funds.

Put one's money on somebody or something: place a bet
He put his money on the sick industry and made it profitable.

Put one's money where one's mouth is: show one's support practically than just talking about it.
Many politicians have big plans but not one of them has been prepared to put his money where his mouth is.

Make money hand over fist: make large profits from a business venture
With their partnership they were able to make money hand over fist.

Money for old rope: money earned with least effort
Money for old rope is possible only theoretically, not practically.

MONTH

In a month of Sundays: for a long time
I have not heard from them in a month of Sundays.

MOON

Many moons ago: long time ago
I met this man many moons ago.

Over the moon: overjoyed
The children were over the moon when they were treated to an ice-cream.

MORE

More and more: increasingly

She is becoming more and more silent with each passing day.

More or less: approximately
She is more or less my height.

More than happy: willingly
I will be more than happy to show you the way to her house.

MOTHBALLS

In mothballs: stored away for long periods
At the natural history museum, rare artifacts were kept in mothballs.

MOUNT

Mount guard at: guard something
The policemen were mounting guard at the political meeting.

MOUTH

Keep one's mouth shut: be secretive or not revealing
He kept his mouth shut about the theft.

Take the words out of someone's mouth: say the same thing the other person wants to say
You took the words out of my mouth when you said that he was a cheat.

Down in the mouth: sad or dejected
He was down in the mouth after his business failed miserably.

MOVE

Make a move: start or begin
We made our moves when it was dark.

On the move: moving
As he is always on the move, it is difficult to meet him.

Move heaven and earth: do everything possible
We had to move heaven and earth to evict the man from our premises.

Move the goal posts: change the pattern of certain matters that are generally accepted.
We have to move the goal posts if we have to bring about a change in the organisation.

MUCH

Not much of a: not a good something
He is not much of a cook but he can manage to cook a decent meal.

As much: equally
We love maths as much as we love science.

MUCK

In muck: very disorganised or untidy
Her kitchen is always in a muck.

MUD

Throw mud at someone: tarnish someone's reputation.
Since she was not reciprocating he decided to throw mud at her reputation.

MUG

A mug's game: an enterprise that may not be successful or profitable
Trying to salvage what is left of the wreck will be a mug's game.

MUSIC

Music to one's ears: soothing or pleasing to one's ears
The news about her winning the election was music to our ears.

MUTTON

Mutton dressed as lamb: elderly person dressed in a youngster's garb.
Mutton dressed as lamb is a suitable way to describe the seventy-year-old man.

MYSELF

All by myself: without help; single handedly
I decided to embark on the journey all by myself.

N

NAIL

Nail one's colours to the mast: declare one's ideas of support openly
She nailed her colours to the mast when she told the class who she supported.

Nail a lie: prove that a statement is wrong
To prove that he is wrong we have to nail a lie to all his statements in the courtroom.

NAKED

The naked eye: view without the help of any objects like a microscope, telescope, etc.
We were able to spot the planet with our naked eyes.

NAME

By the name of: named
He is known by the name of John to all his close friends.

Enter one's name: apply or give in the name for
He entered his name for all the competitions.

Make a name for oneself: become well known or famous
He made a name for himself in the political circles at a very young age.

Under the name of something: use a different name
His articles are always under the name of Edward.

To name a few: give examples
The party was a grand one and many politicians, actors, actresess were there, to name a few.

Take somebody's name in vain: use someone's name ungraciously
She took her husband's name in vain though she was at fault.

NARROW

A narrow squeak: escape by a whisker
It was a narrow squeak when we just managed to jump out of the car before it crashed.

NATURE

Against nature: immoral or unnatural
It is against nature to commit murder.

NEAR

A near miss: just escaped a mishap
When our car hit the tree all of us inside had a near miss.

Nowhere near: far from
The quality of food in this restaurant is nowhere near the food we cook at home.

NECK

Put one's neck on the line: risk one's job for safety
I had to put my neck on the line when my mother was bedridden.

NEED

If need be: if necessary
If need be I can loan you that money you require.

Do the needful: do what is required
When the candidate comes to you please do the needful.

NEEDLE

Give someone the needle: irritate or irk someone
Her inquisitive nature gives me the needle.

NEW

As good as new: in a proper condition
This shoe is as good as new once you clean it.

A new deal: new venture
The two business houses struck a new deal to strengthen their friendship.

Turn over a new leaf: change for the better
He decided to turn over a new leaf and make a name for himself.

NIBS

His nibs: someone who thinks he is above all
His nibs cant think of travelling by an ordinary car.

NICETY

To a nicety: accurate
She calculated the risk we were taking to a nicety.

NICK

In good nick: in good shape or condition
She is middle aged but in good nick.

NIGHT

All night: throughout the night
The friends decided to party all night long.

At night: during night
We cannot see many creatures at night due to darkness.

A late night: keeping awake at night much beyond bed time
Late nights are a way of life for him since he is single.

Day and night: continuously
Day and night the noise continued to bother the neighbourhood.

NIP

Nip and tuck: situation where there is a close contest
In this race it was nip and tuck all the way for the drivers.

NOSE

By a nose: small difference
She lost the first place by a nose.

Have one's nose in something: concentrate while reading
She had a nose in the story book and was not aware of the time passing by.

On the nose: accurately
By telling the truth you have given a message on the nose.

Right under one's nose: right in front of
She had the guts to tell a lie right under my nose.

Cut off one's nose to spite one's face: hurt or injure oneself trying to hurt another

Do not try to cut off your nose to spite your parents, for the result is you will get nowhere.

Keep one's nose clean: not indulge in anything illegal or bad
We decided to keep our nose clean though our friends thought otherwise.

Put one's nose out of joint: insult or embarrass
She did not accept the man's proposal, and it put his nose out of joint.

NOTE

Strike a note: express feelings or voice opinions
The recent political coup struck a note of discontentment among the public.

NOTHING

For nothing: for no reason
She decided to leave her home for nothing.

Nothing like: different
Her appearance is nothing like her character.

Nothing more than: only
The call was nothing more than a mere reminder of the loan he had to pay.

Bring something to someone's notice: inform someone of something
The teacher brought the news of the child's absence to the notice of the principal.

Take no notice: ignore
She took no notice of the people staring at her.

NOTICE

Be beneath one's notice: something that needs to be ignored
She considered the job as beneath her notice.

NOW

Now and then: once in a while; occasionally
He makes a visit to the orphanage now and then.

NUT

Do one's nut: be very annoyed
He is does his nut when he sees the office in a mess.

O

OAR

Stick one's oar in: interfere
He always sticks his oar in when not needed.

Rest on one's oars: rest after a hard day
He deserves to rest his oars after slogging at the office .

OATH

Under oath: swear to tell the truth in court.
As he was under oath he could not cheat on the lawyers.

Take an oath: swear to tell the truth
Before he took charge as the leader he was to take an oath to protect the people.

OBLIGATION

Be under no obligation: not duty bound or not required to
We are under no obligation to visit her relatives.

OBSERVATION

Keep under observation: being monitored carefully
The patient was asked to be kept under strict observation till the doctor returned.

OCCASION

On the occasion of something: during an event
On the occasion of his fiftieth birthday, he threw a big party.

ODD

The odd one out: someone or something remains when the rest are grouped or paired
She is always trying to be the odd one out in the group when we have to go out.

ODDS

Against all odds: despite all oppositions or setbacks
Against all odds he decided to continue his studies.

Be at odds: disagree or quarrel
He is at odds with his boss all the time.

Odds and ends: trinkets or small things
The odds and ends accumulated in this iron chest is 50 years old.

OFF

Off and on: now and then
We keep meeting each other off and on.

OFFER

Offer one's hand: handshake for friendship
Though they were competitors he offered his hand as a sign of friendship.

An offer: sale price reduced
There is an offer on all the food items in the store.

OFFICE

Lay down office: resign from a post.
After thirty five years of service laying down office was a difficult task for him.

Through somebody's kind office: with the help or influence of someone.
Through the manager's kind office we were able to move our files very fast.

OFTEN

As often as: frequently
We visit the temples as often as we can.

OIL PAINTING

Be no oil-painting: be no good looker; be plain
She was no oil-painting but she was very efficient in her job.

OLD

For old times' sake: for memories of the past
For old times' sake let us meet at the same place we met twenty years ago.

The good old days: happy memories
We were taught to be self-sufficient in the good old days.

As old as the hills: ancient
The books in the attic are as old as the hills.

Old enough to know better: be at an age where you need to be more mature and sensible.
You are old enough to know better than to throw a tantrum for silly reasons.

An old wives' tale: silly beliefs or blind faith
It is wise to act practically than to believe in an old wives' tale.

Settle an old score: take revenge
To settle an old score he went searching for the long lost relatives.

An old head on young shoulders: mature beyond age
The girl is still in school, but she has an old head on young shoulders.

An old trout: ill-tempered old person
She is an old trout and prefers to stay alone.

ONCE

All at once: suddenly
All at once we had to repay a huge sum of money to the bank.

At once: immediately
When the salary package was announced the employees rejected it at once.

For once: on a particular occasion
She told the truth for once during the interview.

Once in a blue moon: very rarely
He visited his parents once in a blue moon.

Once more: again or one more time
Please do this exercise once more.

Once upon a time: at a time in the past
Once upon a time there lived a beautiful princess.

ONE

All in one: combined
These exercises are stress busters, therapeutic, healthy—all in one.

One after another: first one person, then another
They stood in a line one after another.

One and only: solely
He is the one and only boy in our class.

OPEN

Be an open secret: known to many though not publicised
It is an open secret that they eloped and got married.

Have an open mind: willing to listen to new ideas
He is a good boss because he has an open mind to all the problems of the staff.

In the open air: outdoors
We pitched tents in the open air and had a great picnic.

Keep one's ears/eyes open: be alert to hear or see something
Keep your ears and eyes open to all the happenings in the courtroom.

An open book: very easy person to know
He is like an open book—very frank and easy in his outlook.

Throw something open: make something available
The landlords have thrown open their fields open to the children to play.

With open arms: happily or enthusiastically
We welcomed the winning team with open arms.

Open one's eye: make one realise
She opened my eyes about his bad characters.

Keep open house: a home open to visitors at all times
Ours is an open house and you are welcome at any time of the day.

OPERATIVE

Operative word: most important word
The teacher has been crying hoarse over it—the operative word being'hoarse'.

OVERPLAY

Overplay one's hand: get into risky situations
She overplayed her hands on his affections for too long.

OPINION

Have a good /bad opinion: think highly or badly of someone or something
We have a very good opinion about this institution.

In my opinion: in my view

In my opinion he is a cheat.

ORDER

Be under orders: instructed to do something
He was under orders not to show the files to anyone.

In working order: working smoothly
The machines in this factory are maintained well and are in good working order.

Out of order: not in working condition
The ice-cream vending machine was out of order.

Made to order: according to customer specification
This piece of jewellery is made to order by a customer.

ORDINARY

In the ordinary way: normal or usual way
Things would have happened the ordinary way but for the strike of the employees.

Out of the ordinary: unusual
Her sense of dressing is out of the ordinary but her behaviour is nothing to talk about.

Be out to do something: hoping or trying to do something
The girls were out to impress all the boys in the college.

Out and about: recouped after an illness
He is out and about after the attack of malaria.

OVERSHOOT

Overshoot the mark: error caused due to misjudgement of a particular person or situation
We overshot the mark of trusting a new employee to give a good presentation.

OWN

Hold one's own: carry on against all odds
She decided to hold her own even though the whole family did not support her.

On one's own: alone; single-handedly
He decided to embark on the dangerous route on his own.

P

PACE

Keep pace with: keep the same tempo or speed
It is very difficult to keep pace with his style of working.

Set the pace: start a trend or way of functioning which others can follow
Once she took over as the head of the department she set the pace of working in a very systematic way.

PACK

Pack one's bag: ready one's bag
She packed her bags and got ready to leave her husband's house.

Pack a punch: deliver a powerful message.
In her last meeting she packed a punch in her vote of thanks.

PAIN

A pain in the neck: irritating or annoying
My new neighbour is a pain in the neck.

Take great pains over something: take great effort or care over something
She takes great pains to please all her relatives.

PAIR

In pairs: in twos or a couple
We are supposed to attend the party only in pairs.

PALE

Beyond the pale: generally not accepted
Her behaviour is always beyond the pale of the family tradition.

PALM

Have one in the palm of one's hand: control someone
With her charm she is able to have her family in the palm of her hands.

PANIC

Panic stations: state of alarm
It was panic stations when the new government was overthrown in a few days.

PAR

Below par: less well, alert, etc. than usual
The quality of all the jewellery is below par than the value mentioned.

On par with someone or something: equal to
After this promotion his status is on par with all his seniors.

PARADE

Make a parade of something: a show off
She is always making a parade of all her jewellery.

PARISH

Parish pump: local politics
She is always getting involved with parish pumps in the locality.

PART

The best part of something: the better section or chunk
We spend the best part of our lives in school.

Look the part: look like the role you play
The young girl in the play looked the part.

For the most part: by and large, all in all
You can safely invest with the company as for most part they are reliable.

On the part of somebody: made by or done by
It was a big blunder on the part of the manager.

In part: partially; to some extent
His success is due in part to good luck.

Take part in: participate or join in
I wish to take part in the school play.

Part with someone/something: give up; forgo
I had to part with the family heirloom to tide over the financial crisis.

PASS

Come to pass: happen, occur
It came to pass that the old man died.

Come to a pretty pass: come to crucial state or critical state
Things have come to a pretty pass that they have to sell the house.

Make a pass at: make a sexual approach
The boss tried to make a pass at his secretary.

PAT

Pat somebody or oneself: compliment or applaud
He patted himself on the back for bringing off the deal.

PATCH

Go through a bad patch: have bad spell or bad period
We had to go through a bad patch initially when the business was started.

PATTER

The patter of tiny feet: the sounds of little children around the house
She missed the patter of tiny feet when her grandchildren went back home.

PAY

Pay attention: heed or listen carefully
We have to pay attention to all the instructions given to us.

Pay somebody a compliment: praise someone
When the play was over the chief guest paid a compliment to the entire cast.

Pay dividends: give results or gains
Investing in this new company is paying us rich dividends.

Pay back in the same coin: tit for tat
She was cheated by her husband and decided to pay him back in the same coin.

Pay the price: suffer the consequences
We have to pay the price for all our actions.

Pay through the nose: pay more than necessary; very expensive
He paid through his nose for the diamond ring.

Pay court to somebody: be nice to someone in order to get a favour
He believes in paying court to all his seniors in order to get a promotion.

PEACE

Hold one's peace: keep quiet in spite of wanting to give one's opinion
I had to hold my peace when there was a family conflict.

PEAK

Peak and pine: fall sick due to mental agony
He peaked and pined after his separation from the children.

PEBBLE

Not the only pebble on the beach: not be the only person who matters
He must get it into his head that he is not the only pebble on the beach to achieve this feat.

PEDESTAL

Put on a pedestal: flatter someone
They have put the new manager on a pedestal; let us see how he functions.

PENNY

The penny drops: come to understand something which was difficult to understand
The teacher had to teach the lesson again to the students before the penny dropped.

Turn up like a bad penny: an unwelcome guest
I did not want to turn up like a bad penny at the new year's party.

PERIL

At one's peril: at one's risk
Despite all warnings he decided to trek the mountain at his own peril.

In peril of one's life: danger of death
The stuntman was always ready to take risks despite the peril of his life.

PERSON

On one's person: have with oneself
An old diary was found on his person.

In person: physically present
You must collect the tickets in person before the show.

PHRASE

Turn a phrase: express with a sense of humour
By turning a phrase, he was able to keep the party alive.

Turn of phrase: distinct way of describing certain things.
The teacher made the class interesting by a turn of phrase that caught the attention of the children.

Pick holes in something: find fault with something
He loves to pick holes in all that his wife does.

PICK

Pick and choose: be fussy
She spends hours before her wardrobe picking and choosing her dress.

Pick a fight: cause a fight on purpose
The boy on the street picked up a fight with the man to squeeze some money out of him.

Pick somebody's pocket: steal from someone's pocket
Beware of the beggar as he is always picking someone's pockets.

PICTURE

Get the picture: understand
Now that I've seen the situation, I get the picture.

Put someone in the picture: keep someone abreast with the developments
He was away on tour for three months and I put him in the picture about the events in the office.

Be the picture of health: have a healthy outlook
Though he is sixty years old, he is a picture of health.

PIE

Pie in the sky: a turn of event that is unlikely to happen in the near future.
His ambition of building houses to all his workers is just a pie in the sky.

PIECE

Give somebody a piece of one's mind: advise someone frankly of his faults

Looking at her behaviour I decided to give her a piece of my mind.

In one piece: unharmed
After the accident we returned home in one piece.

Pull somebody to pieces: criticise someone in their absence
Knowing well the manager was on leave we pulled him to pieces.

Piece by piece: bit by bit
We solved the puzzle piece by piece.

A piece of cake: very easy task
Solving these problems was a piece of cake.

PIG

Make a pig's ear out of something: something not done properly
I asked her to complete the project and she made a pig's ear out of it.

Pigs might fly: miracles that may or may not occur
Pigs might fly but this construction work cannot be completed by next week.

PILE

Make a pile: earn loads of money
He made a pile by selling all his stocks.

Pile it on: exaggerate
His reputation is not bad as she says—she does tend to pile it on.

PINCH

Pinch and save: spend money in a tight-fisted way
They always pinched and saved, and missed out on all good things in life.

If it comes to the pinch: if an emergency arises
If it comes to the pinch we can always sell the house

PINK

In the pink of health: very good health condition
She was in the pink of health and was able to deliver the twins.

PIP

Give someone the pip: instigate a feeling of anger or depression
Her morose nature gives us all the pips.

Pip somebody at the post: have a narrow win
He pipped the world champion by a few seconds.

PIPING

Piping hot: very hot
We felt like having a piping hot drink in the cold weather.

PITY

More's the pity: unluckily
More's the pity when we have to sell off the property to pay our loans.

PLACE

Swap places with: exchange positions or situations
When I heard that she got a job abroad I wished I could swap places with her.

Go places: become very successful
After completion of his Masters' degree he is sure to go places.

In the first place: firstly
In the first place let me brief you about the rules of the game.

In your place: in your situation or position
If I were in your place I would have dealt with him in a rude manner.

In place: in order
He makes sure that his tools are always in place after his job.

In place of somebody: instead of somebody
We will hire you in place of your sister.

Put oneself in somebody's place: imagine yourself in another's situation or position
Put yourself in her place and see what hardships she has to go through with her husband.

Put someone in his place: cut someone down to size, humiliate
When he tried to flirt with her she put him in his place.

Take place: occur, or happen
Where did the murder take place?

Out of place: not in order, out of position
She felt out of place amidst all his relatives.

PLAIN

Make oneself plain: be very clear
You cannot speak to strangers in the train—do I make myself plain?

PLATE

Give someone something on a plate: give something to somebody with an effort on their part
You can't expect success to be given to you on a plate when you have not been lifted a finger to help in the project.

PLEASURE

Have the pleasure of doing something: used to make polite requests
Please have the pleasure of of your company.

With pleasure: pleased to do something
I will tell the children stories with pleasure.

PLENTY

In plenty: in great quantity
Vegetables were available in plenty at all the road corners.

PLIGHT

Plight one's tooth: a promise to wed somebody
He had to plight his tooth to his girlfriend before she went out with him.

PLOUGH

Plough a lonely furrow: work single-handedly
She had to plough a lonely furrow to support her kids.

Pluck up courage: try to be brave
I had to pluck up courage to face my boss when I took leave without pemission.

PLUMB

Plumb the depth of something: get to the lowest point of something
We have to plumb the lowest depth of this problem to find a solution.

POCKET

Be in somebody's pocket: be very close with somebody
You can always find them in each other's pocket.

Pocket one's pride: suppress one's anger or feelings
Pocketing his pride he went up to her and apologised.

Have someone in one's pocket: control someone
We had to have the workers in our pocket before starting anything new.

POINT

At the point of a gun: threaten at gun point
The thief made away with all the valuables at the point of a gun.

Carry one's point: convince people to accept one's argument or decision
The leader carried his point to all the workers to gain their confidence.

Have one's points: have advantages
No doubt Science has its points but I still prefer the Arts.

When it comes to the point: ultimately
When it comes to the point of choosing between friends and relatives I will settle for friends.

Make one's point: be very clear about one's idea
She made her point very clear to the team before starting the project.

On the point of doing something: just about to do something
We were on the point of leaving the house when the guests arrived.

The point of no return: a point where decisions or actions cannot be reversed.
When she married the actor, it was a point of no return.

To the point: very minimal or what is exactly required.
The chief guest's speech was to the point and informative.

Point the finger at: accuse someone
When the mission failed all fingers pointed at the leader of the mission.

POSITION

In position: in order or in place
All the books were in position before the inspection.

POSSESS

Be possessed of something: have a particular quality
She is possessed with a great quality of patience.

Like one possessed: violently or overcome with madness
When he heard that his son died he ran like a man possessed.

POUR

Pour oil on the flames: worsen a bad situation
You should not pour oil on the flames when you know she is already depressed.

POWDER

Keep one's powder dry: be prepared for any emergencies
We are saved from the rains this season but it is better to keep one's powder dry.

POWER

In power: having control or authority
His father's party was in power during the elections.

The real power behind the throne: the real person controlling
The real power behind the throne is the vice president.

Powers that be: people who control an organisation, country, etc.
The personal assistant is waiting for the powers that be to decide on his future.

PREACH

Preach to the converted: talk to people about the same view they hold
Do not preach to the converted and waste your time.

PREPARE

Be prepared to do something: willing to do something
He was prepared to feed all the poor students in the school.

Be prepared for something: be ready for some happening
We were very well prepared for the floods.

PRESENCE

In the presence of somebody: in front of somebody
In the presence of the staff he fired the teacher.

Make one's presence felt: make other aware of one's presence by one's personality
The world cup champions made their presence felt in the tournament this year too.

Presence of mind: ability of being alert or quick thinking
Due to her presence of mind she was able to save her husband's life.

PRESENT

The present day: the modern times
The present day meaning of marriage is convenience.

At present: now
At present she is staying with her parents.

PRESS

Be pressed for something: have very little of something
I am always pressed for time in the morning hours.

Press someone into service: use something as it is urgently needed
An ambulance was pressed into service at the accident site.

PRESSURE

Put pressure on somebody: force somebody
She put pressure on her husband to take her on a vacation.

Under pressure: stress
They were under pressure to complete the assignment in two days.

PRETTY

Pretty as a picture: very good looking
Her daughter is pretty as a picture.

Pretty much: almost
These two curries are pretty much the same taste.

PRICE

At a price: costly
He bought her a ring—at a price!

At any price: whatever the cost
I am willing to buy this house at any price.

Put a price on something: value something in terms of money
You cannot put a price on hard work.

PRIDE

Pride of place: the most important position
This necklace has a pride of place in my collection of Jewellery.

Somebody's pride and joy: something that makes a person proud
This little piano was her pride and joy.

Take pride in: be keen and proud to do something
He takes pride in his collection of music.

PROPORTION

In proportion: equally distributed
The house plan is not in proportion to other things in the drawings given.

Out of all proportions: too huge or too serious
The supply for uniforms is out of all proportions to the number of sets required.

PROVE

Prove one's point: establish that one's argument or statement is true
To prove his point he made an elaborate survey and submitted it to the authorities.

PROWL

On the prowl: move about or stalk
The thieves were prowling around the grounds looking for a way into the building.

PSYCHOLOGY

The psychological moment: right opportunity to reap success
It was a psychological moment to ask the boss for a raise.

PUBLIC

Go public: sell shares to the public and become a public company
The prospects of the company looked good once they went public.

In the public eye: well known to the public
If he has to win the elections he has to be in the public eye for a while.

In public: openly; not in private
He had a fight with his wife in public.

PULL

Pull a fast one on somebody: trick one's way or lie to escape
She pulled a fast one and escaped from the meeting.

Pull somebody's leg: tease or make fun of
She was upset but he was only pulling her leg.

Pull one's socks up: improve one's position with extra efforts
She decided to pull up her socks and study hard for the exams.

Pull strings: use influence
He decided to pull strings and get his daughter a seat in the college.

Pull the wool over one's eyes: outwit someone
You cannot pull the wool over the seventy-year-old lady and make an escape.

Pull out all stops: use influence to reach a goal
They pulled out all stops to ensure that he got a seat in the prestigious college.

PURSUIT

In pursuit of someone: chase someone
The police were in pursuit of the thief for almost a week.

In pursuit of something: goal or aim of obtaining something
He gave up his life's pleasures in pursuit of a career in medicine.

PUSH

Be pushed for something: not have enough of something
They were pushed for time before the wedding.

Push one's luck: take risks banking on good luck to hold out
Don't push your luck too far this time as the paper may be very tough.

PUT

Not put it past somebody to do something: underestimate someone's strength.
I wouldn't put it past him to do very well in the exams as he is preparing very well.

Put somebody through it: force someone into an unpleasant situation
We have to put the youngsters through the grind before they actually taste power.

Put together: combined
We put together all our resources and started this company.

Put the fear of God into somebody: make someone afraid to a great extent
We had to put the fear of God into the students to make them work harder.

Put the flags out: celebrate to a happy cause
We put the flags out and decided to celebrate his rare victory in the Olympics.

Put a quarter into a pint pot: try to cram something big into a smaller area
He was trying to put a quarter into a pint pot when he tried to fit the chair into the car seat.

Put a sock in it: stop talking or making a noise
The children were arguing for a long time when the father put a sock in it.

Put somebody through the wringer: put someone in an awkward position
I was put through a wringer when I was pulled up for the failure of the project.

Put someone on a pedestal: a belief about a person that he or she is perfect.
Everyday in my life I put my mother on a pedestal and try to be like her.

Put a person on the mill: subject someone to a tough test
He was put on the mill when he was asked to give a presentation that he was not prepared for.

PUTTY

Be putty in somebody's hands: be easily influenced by someone
She was a woman of such beauty and charm that men were putty in her hands.

Q

QUEEN

Queen it: behave as if in power
Ever since she was elected the captain she queens it over all the players.

QUESTION

Come into question: point to be discussed or pondered over
The rise in the salary brings into question the role of each employee in the company.

Out of question: impossible or unthinkable
The possibility of sending the children without an adult is out of question.

QUID

Quids in: in a position to profit from something
As their sales have soared they are now quids in.

QUICK

Quick as lightning: very quickly
She is quick as lightning in her replies.

Quick off the mark: a prompt start
When the whistle blew, the athletes were quick off the mark.

QUIET

Keep quiet about: keep in secrecy or say nothing
He has kept quiet about the disturbances in the office.

On the quiet: secretly

They have been meeting each other on the quiet .

QUITS

Be quits with somebody: get even with someone
When you return the money you borrowed from me we will be quits.

QUITE

Quite a few: reasonable quantity
Quite a few members attended the meeting.

Quite some time: reasonable length of time
It is quite some time since I saw my sister.

R

RACE

Race against time: hurry or hasten

Every morning it is a race against time when we have to send the kids to school.

RACK

Rack one's brains: think hard

We have to rack our brains hard before we can answer the questions of little children.

RAIN

Come rain or shine: whether it rains or there is sunshine

We will go swimming today, come rain or shine.

Take a rain check: agree to take an offer at a later date

Thanks for the proposal , but let me take a rain check on it.

Rain cats and dogs: pour heavily

It rains cats and dogs in the month of July.

RAISE

Raise hell: cause an uproar or show of anger

He raised hell when he found that the project was not completed on time.

Raise one's eyebrow: show of surprise

He raised his eyebrow when he saw her new outfit.

Raise one's glass to something: drink to or toast to something
We decided to raise our glass to the profit we made in the exhibition.

Raise somebody's spirit: cheer up somebody
We decided to raise the sick child's spirit by playing the games he liked.

Raise the temperature: increase the tension or hostility
He raised the temperature in the office with his comments on the management.

Raise one's voice against something or someone: protest
She raised her voice against the ill treatment meted out to her.

RAGTAG

Ragtag and bobtail: dishonourable people
They are a bunch of ragtag and bobtail people and deserve no mercy.

RAKE

Rake over old ashes: revive old memories
I do not wish to rake over the old ashes and spoil my future.

RAMROD

Straight as a ramrod: stiff or erect
The soldiers stood straight as a ramrod in front of the commander.

RANDOM

At random: unmethodical or casually
She alway chooses her clothes at random.

RAP

Get a rap on the knuckles: get rebuked
She got a rap on the knuckles for not finishing her homework.

Take the rap: take the blame
He had to take the rap for the misbehaviour of all the students.

RAT

Rat race: fierce competition
We are all in a rat race to achieve something .

RATE

At any rate: in any case; anyhow
At any rate we are going to be late for the party.

At this rate: if this continues
At this rate he will be a pauper very soon.

REACH

Reach for the stars: be very ambitious
We have to study well and always aim for the stars.

Within one's reach: capable of attaining or getting
The boxes on the attic are within his reach.

READ

Read between lines: assume or infer more than what is there
He always reads between lines and comes to the wrong conclusions.

Read someone like a book: gauge someone correctly
He has the ability to read people like a book .

Take it as read: accept something without a discussion
You can take his agreement as read.

REAL

For real: genuine
I do not think his intentions are for real.

REASON

Beyond all reason: unreasonable
His argument is beyond all reason.

For reason best known to oneself: reasons that others cannot understand
For reasons best known to himself he did not attend the party.

Within reason: in moderation or sensible limits
We will do anything within reason to bring peace at home.

REBOUND

On the rebound: as a result of
When the child was picked up for not cleaning his room, he threw up a tantrum on the rebound.

RECORD

For the record: for the sake of accuracy
Just for the record his name was involved in the match fixing scam.

On record: registered or officially noted

This is the wettest winter on record.

A track record: achievements
His track record as an able minister is know to one and all.

Off the record: unofficial; not publicised
This information about the murder is off the record.

Set the record straight: clear the misunderstanding
He decided to set the record straight by personally approaching the manager.

REDEMPTION

Beyond redemption: past the stage of recovery
She is so used to telling a lie that she is beyond redemption.

REFERENCE

Bear no reference to something: have no relation to something
This has no reference to the article in the newspaper.

With reference to someone or something: with regard to
With reference to your note I am making necessary changes.

REFRESH

Refresh one's memory: recall or remind
Please refresh my memory with the names of all our old classmates.

RELATION

With relation to someone or something: concerning someone or something
He is always travelling abroad with relation to his work.

REQUEST

At the request of: at the wish of someone
We attended the wedding at the request of the bride.

On request: when needed
Tickets for the film are available on request.

RESPECT

With respect to something: with relevance or regard to something
With respect to the matter in hand he approached the principal.

REST

Rest assured that: be sure that

Be rest assured that he will accompanied with his mother.

At rest: without motion
The body lay at rest in the mortuary.

Come to rest: stop or halt
The bus came to a rest at the road junction.

Lay someone to rest: bury someone
The man was laid to rest with full honours.

RESTRAINT

Without restraint: without barriers
We all cried without restraint when we saw the touching scene in the movie.

RETURN

Return to the fold: rejoin a group with similar beliefs
After years of working hard he decided to return to the fold of the religious group.

By return (of post): by next post.
I am waiting for his letter by return of post.

REVERSE

In reverse order: from the end to the beginning
We played all the songs in reverse order.

Reverse the charges: telephonic calls charged to the receiver
He was instructed to reverse the charges of all the calls he made.

REVERT

Revert to type: go back to normal condition
It is high time the students revert to type after two months of vacation.

RHAPSODY

Go into rhapsodies over somebody: express willingness or delight in speech or writing
We went into rhapsodies when we were given the weekend off.

RHINOCEROS

Skin like a rhinoceros: person with a hard heart
He has skin like a rhinoceros, and will not yield to anything.

RHYME

Without any rhyme or reason: illogical
His anger at the staff is without any rhyme or reason.

RICH

Rich as Croesus: very wealthy
He is rich as Croesus and knows how to make more wealth.

RIDE

Ride at anchor: be secured by the anchor
He had to ride at anchor for four hours before help came.

Take someone for a ride: fool someone
We were taken for a ride by the guide at the museum.

RIGHT

All right: used to indicate agreement or approval
All right, we can go for a movie tonight.

Do the right thing: do the correct thing
He did the right thing by taking her to court.

Set something right: put something in order
She set the classroom right by keeping all the children occupied with stories.

Right now: immediately
I am going to meet him right now.

In one's own right: personal qualification
She is a great singer in her own right.

Right and left: everywhere
He borrowed money right and left to lead a luxurious life.

RING

Run rings round somebody: perform better than others
His show in the exams always ran rings round all the other students of the class.

Ring a bell: remind or be able to recollect
His name certainly rings a bell in all the literary circles.

RISE

Take a rise out of somebody: irritate or annoy a person
He took a rise out of her by calling her a fool.

Give rise to something: lead to something
His actions have given rise to many rifts in the organization.

Rise and shine: wake up and be active
Its already 9 am; rise and shine!

RISK

At one's own risk: take a chance on your own
If you are going to climb that hill, do so at your own risk.

At risk: at stake or in danger
The brave man put his life at risk to save the people from drowning.

Take a risk: take a chance or venture into something
We had to take the risk of getting onto the train though we had no reservations.

ROAD

By road: travel by any vehicle like a car, bus, cycle, etc.
We decided to go to the resort by road.

On the road: travelling
He read up the files while travelling to office by bus.

The road to something: towards a particular direction
The road to success is hard work.

One for the road: last drink before leaving
He had to have one for the road before leaving for the party.

ROAR

Do a roaring trade: sell fast
He did a roaring trade when he decided to sell off his furniture.

A roaring success: great achievement; success
The play was a roaring success.

ROCK

On the rocks: not steady
Their marriage was on the rocks from the very beginning.

Solid as a rock: tower of strength, anchor
He is solid as a rock and dependable in times of trouble.

ROLL

Be rolling in money: have lots of money

She is rolling in money and does not know the value of it.

Rolled into one: combined into one
She is a writer and a painter rolled into one.

Rolling in the aisles: helpless with laughter
The clown had the children rolling in the aisles.

Roll up one's sleeves: get ready to do a certain task
We all rolled up our sleeves to clean the campus.

Roll in: gather in large numbers
As the new movie was released the people rolled in to see the first show.

ROOTS

Get to the roots of something: get to the cause or source of something
He decided to get to the root of the problem of the workers before firing them.

The root cause: the main cause
The root cause of her illness is her eating habit.

ROPE

Give someone plenty of rope: give someone plenty of chance or freedom
Give someone plenty of rope and he will soon master the art.

Learn the ropes: learn the tricks of the trade or rules of the game
I decided to learn the ropes of management in the absence of the manager.

ROUGH

Be rough on somebody: treat someone harshly or be unrelenting
He was very rough on his old parents.

Have a rough time: have difficult or cruel times
They had a rough time in the initial years of starting their business.

A rough estimate: approximate; vague
We have given a rough estimate of the construction.

ROUNDS

Do the rounds: tour or go around a place
We did the rounds of all the temples in the city.

ROW

In a row: placed one after another
We stood in a row to witness the demonstration.

RUB

Rub salt into one's wounds: rekindle or remind one of the bad experiences.
He rubbed salt into her wounds by asking about her busband.

Rub shoulders with somebody: get to meet people professionally.
In his line of job he gets to rub shoulders with all the actors and actresses.

Rub somebody the wrong way: irritate or irk somebody.
He always rubs people the wrong way with his impolite behaviour.

RUIN

In ruins: in bad condition
Their ancestral home is in ruins.

RULE

As a rule: normally
As a rule he always comes to work on time.

Rules of the road: points to be remembered while driving vehicles on road.
The rules of the road help you to have a safe journey.

Rule the roost: be in charge or in control
Wherever he goes he will rule the roost.

Rule with an iron hand: be an authoritative ruler.
The minister was able to rule with an iron hand.

RUN

The common run: the average type or class
This is a hotel out of the ordinary run.

Run for it: try to escape
Run for it before the police catch up with you!

On the run: active and always moving about.
Though she is seventy she is always on the run.

Run before you can walk: try complicated things before learning the basic
Though you are intelligent you have to run before you can walk.

Run out of steam: put an abrupt end to something that you are doing continuously
In the middle of completing the house hold chores, I ran out of steam and took a nap.

A dummy run: a trial before the actual show/performance
We did a dummy run of the play in the auditorium to get the feel of the stage.

Run something up the flagpole: reveal something to get a public feedback
We ran the prepole survey about the candidates one week before the elections

RUT

Be in a rut: a normal and boring routine
I am sick of being in a rut all my life.

S

SACK

Sack cloth and ashes: in a state of mourning
We were still in sack cloth and ashes when we were asked to vacate the house.

SAFE

For safe keeping: to be kept securely or undamaged
You can leave all your jewels with me for safe keeping.

Play it safe: avoid all risks, or be very careful
To play it safe we always invest in government bonds.

Safe and sound: out of danger or unharmed
We reached our destination safe and sound.

A safe bet: sure of success
Voting for the ruling party is a safe bet.

Safe as houses: protected or guarded
We can stand under this tree which is safe as houses.

SAIL

Set sail: start a voyage by ship or boat
They set sail from Chennai to Andamans.

Under sail: with sails spread
The boats were under sail for the long voyage.

SALT

Salt of the earth: honest or honourable person or people
She is the salt of the earth and can be entrusted with any job.

SAME

Come to be the same thing: not different
Whether you watch this movie or that it comes to the same thing.

At the same time: together or side by side
We all went to the theatre at the same time.

Be in the same boat: be in a similar situation
We are in the same boat since both of us have lost our wallets.

Be of the same mind: think alike
We are of the same mind, hence we get along so well!

In the same breadth: immediately after saying something
He yelled at her for her carelessness but in the same breadth praised her for the truthfulness.

One and the same: something or someone alike
Going to their house or inviting them to our house is one and the same.

SAND

The sands are running out: have very little time
The sands are running out and we have to finish this job before the boss arrives tomorrow.

SARDINE

Squashed like sardines: placed close together
We were squashed like sardines in the crowded public transport bus.

SAUCE

In the sauce: drunk
He was in the sauce when his children went to speak to him.

SAUSAGE

Not a sausage: nothing at all
We did not get a sausage for all the work we did for him.

SAVE

Save somebody's bacon: prevent someone from being harmed
She would have nearly been killed if he had not intervened and saved her bacon.

Save one's breath: refrain from speaking when it does not serve the purpose.
You can save your breath as she is not going to take advice from anyone.

Save somebody's face: keep one's pride or reputation
She saved my face when she conceded the match to me.

Save one's skin: escape from danger or harm
We decided to save our skins by abandoning the vehicle and walking home.

SAY

Go without saying: it is obvious
It goes without saying that we must treat our teachers with respect.

The less said the better: say little or nothing
The less said the better about his behaviour.

Let us say: for example
Let us say this is the kind of house our ancestors used to live in.

Never say die: not to give up
Never say die—we must not give up the fight.

Say the word: order or wish
Say the word and I will teach him a lesson.

To say the least: talk little about
To say the least this is the best deal we have got.

Have one's say: express one's opinion
He has to have a say in everything she does.

Before you can say Jack Robinson: suddenly or very fast
The rabbit ran away before you could say Jack Robinson.

SCALE

The scales fall from somebody's eyes: realise the truth after being duped
The scales fell from his eyes only after his partner ran away with all the money.

To scale: proportionate or correct size
The architect designed the house to scale.

SCENE

Behind the scenes: secretly
He was asked to give up the fight behind the scenes.

On the scene: present
The cops were on the scene of the crime.

Come on the scene: be present
I did not interfere till he came on the scene.

Not one's scene: not to one's liking
Going by car to a place so close by is not my scene.

SCINTILLA

Not a scintilla of something: not even a smallest quantity of something
There is not a scintilla of doubt that she would be the right candidate for the job.

SCISSORS

Scissors and paste: a compilation of works from different sources
This is definitely a scissors and paste work and needs no second look.

SCRAPE

Scrape up an acquaintance with somebody: getting to know a person with great difficulty
We had to scrape up an acquaintance with the juniors to get the job done on time.

SCRATCH

Scratch one's head: think hard
I scratched my head hard to recollect her name.

Start from scratch: start from the very beginning
They had to start their lives from scratch.

SCRIMP

Scrimp and save: live on a meagre income
We had to scrimp and save for six months before I got a job.

SEA

Over the seas: places on the other side of the seas
The sailor decided to explore the countries over the seas.

Go to sea: become a sailor
I trained for five years to go to sea.

At sea: confused
I am at sea over the questions asked in our exams.

SECOND

Second only to someone or something: having one person or thing more important than the rest
He is second only to my parents in my affections.

Second to none: the very best
The performance of our product is second to none.

SEE

For all the world to see: clear
He made a declaration of his affection for all the world to see.

See for oneself: be convinced
You can see for yourself that he is a big liar.

SEED

Seeds of something: cause or beginning of something
She has sown the seeds of hatred in the family by living separately.

Run to seed: be reckless or careless about the appearance
This bunglow has run to seed since the old lady died.

SELL

Be sold on something: be eager about something
I like her dress but I am not sold over the fact that I have to go so far to buy it.

Sell something/someone short: not realise the true value
Don't sell the poor boy short, he is very talented in same areas.

SENSE

Knock some sense into someone: be able to change someone
I hope his mother will knock some sense into his dumb head.

In one's senses: normal self
He was not in his senses when they had the fight.

Make sense: easy to understand
Her arguments made sense in the courtroom.

See sense: comprehend or think sensibly
I am sure she will see sense and change her opinion.

A sixth sense: intuition
He had a sixth sense that they would be in deep trouble if they followed that route.

Out of one's senses: out of one's mind
You must be out of your senses if you have to give such an idea.

SERVE

Serve somebody right: deserve
It serves him right that all his neighbours ignored him.

Serve one's turn: be utilised for a period of time
We had to replace the old machine since it had served its turn.

SESSION

In session: in progress
The meeting is in session for the past two hours.

SET

Be all set for something: be prepared for something
We were all set to go for the match when it started pouring.

Be set on doing something: determined about doing something
She was set on doing all the domestic chores herself without any help.

SETTLE

To settle one's account: to take revenge or have tit for tat
He was determined to settle an account with her for insulting him in public.

SHAKE

Shake in one's shoes: be scared or frightened
The little boy was shaking in his shoes when his teacher yelled at him.

Shake like a leaf: tremble nervously
I shook like a leaf when my father scolded me.

SHANK

On shank's pony: on foot
I prefer to go to the marker on shank's pony than a car.

SHAPE

Get oneself into shape: exercise to get fit
When I checked my weight today I decided that I had to get into shape very soon.

Give shape to something: give a clear picture
We have been trying to give shape to this project by creating a model.

In shape: very fit
Though she is fifty years old she is in great shape.

In the shape of something: appears to be
He came in the shape of an angel and saved us from further trouble.

Out of shape: disfigured or unfit
When we go out of shape we become very self-conscious.

Take shape: final turnout
His efforts have finally taken shape after so many years.

SHELL

Come out of one's shell: come out and be more expressive
She has to come out of her shell if she has to find a job.

Go into a shell: become reserved and shy
The little girl went into a shell when she was criticised in class.

SHOOT

Shoot a line: exaggerate
He said he was very influential but we knew he was only shooting a line.

Shoot one's mouth off: boast
He has this irritating habit of shooting his mouth off in the most unwanted places.

Shoot one's bolt: one last attempt after everything has been tried
I shot a bolt by directly approaching the official to clear my files that were pending.

Shoot the breeze: gossip casually
We get together every morning to shoot the breeze in the park.

Shoot the works: gamble and squander all the money
At the casino we shot the works and had a good time.

SHOP

Set up shop: start a business or enterprise
He set up shop in most cities to expand his business.

SHORT

For short: as an abbreviation
Her name is Deepika, but Deepa for short.

In short: briefly
In short, she is a very hard-working person.

In short supply: scarce
Air conditioners are in short supply this summer due to the demand.

Nothing short of something: nothing less than something
Their performance was nothing short of perfection.

On a short fuse: quick-tempered
He is always on a short fuse in the mornings.

A short cut: easy way out
There is no short cut to success.

Short and sweet: brief and enjoyable
Out trip this weekend was short and sweet.

SHOT

A shot in the arm: encouragement or stimulus
The new government policy is a shot in the arm for the tourist industry.

Like a shot: willingly or without hesitation
He would take the job like a shot.

SHOW

On show: on display
They had put up a new collection of clothes on show at the exhibition.

Good show: good performance
The children put up a good show at the Christmas programme.

Show somebody the door: ask someone to leave
He was shown the door when he revealed that he was a salesman.

Show the way: lead by example
She showed the way to all the ladies in colony by making a career at home.

SHRINK

A shrinking violet: shy person
She is such a shrinking violet that it is hard to convince her.

SHUT

Shut one's ear to something: refuse to listen to something
We decided to shut our ears to the pleas of the criminals.

Shut the door on something: evade or ignore
When the workers asked for a raise he shut the door on it.

Shut down: cease to operate
As we incurred heavy losses we decided to shut down the factory.

Shut one's mouth: be silent or hold one's tongue
It is better to shut one's mouth than to talk out of turn.

SICK

Fall sick: laid up or unwell
He fell sick on his first business trip.

Make somebody sick: distress or disgust someone
He makes me sick with his uncouth manners.

Sick as a parrot: repelling
His behaviour at the party was sick as a parrot.

On the sick list: absent from duty
He is the seventh person on the sick list this week.

Sick to one's stomach: detestable or gross
I am sick to my stomach when I see his face.

SIDE

Get on the wrong side of someone: irritate someone
He always gets on the wrong side of the boss and gets himself into trouble.

From all sides: from everywhere
She received praise from all sides of the country for her fine performance.

Come down on one side of the fence: be able to make a choice between two alternatives
He has to come down on one side of the fence and choose between his family or his wife.

SIGHT

At sight: view
We were asked to click snaps of the rare birds at sight.

Set sights on something: objective or aim for something
She has set her sights on getting the top honours at the examinations.

A sight for sore eyes: pleasurable sight
The blooming of the roses was a sight for sore eyes in our dried up garden.

SILENT

The silent majority: people who cannot express their views openly
They are a silent majority in the office and have no voice in the promotions.

SILK

Take silk: become a royal advisor
After struggling in the lower ranks for years he has now taken silk.

SILVER

The silver screen: film industry or acting in a movie
As a journalist I get to meet lots of people from the silver screen.

A silver tongue: impressive talker
She manages to get all her work done with her silver tongue.

SINK

Be sunk in something: be deeply involved
He was sunk in his own thoughts and did not hear the car behind him.

Sink one's differences: overlook or disregard
They decided to sink their differences and start a new venture.

A sinking feeling: a low feeling
I have a sinking feeling that we are going to lose the match today.

Sink like a stone: go down immediately
The ring sunk like a stone as soon as it fell into the well.

SIT

Sit at somebody's feet: become a follower of someone
After hearing the Guruji's speech we decided to sit at his feet.

Sit on the fence: be undecided
He is still sitting on the fence with regard to the decision on selling the house.

Sit on one's hand: sit idle
It is not good to sit on one's hand when there is so much to do.

A sitting duck: an easy target to attack
By sitting in front of the door he has become a sitting duck to the manager's wrath.

Sitting pretty: being lucky
He is sitting pretty on all the wealth that his father has earned for him.

Sit up and take notice: get alert and observe what is happening
When the company started going on a loss he decided to sit up and take notice of all the dealings himself.

SIX

At sixes and sevens: a confused state
The whole house is in sixes and sevens since we moved in only yesterday.

SKATE

Be skating on thin ice: talk about a controversial topic that can spark off disagreements.
Her advice is like skating on thin ice and we don't want to risk it.

SKELETON

Skeleton in the cupboard: secrets which revealed can cause trouble
Once he is arrested many skeletons in the cupboard will fall out, and cause more confusion.

SKIN

By the skin of one's teeth: near miss
In the road accident the children were saved by the skin of their teeth.

Have got somebody under one skin: be infatuated or strongly attracted to
It was difficult to forget her as she had got under his skin for the last five years.

Jump out of one's skin: scare or startle
I jumped out of my skin when I heard the sudden roll of thunder.

Skin and bone: skinny or thin
After her diet regime she is nothing but skin and bones.

Soaked to the skin: completely wet
We were soaked to the skin when we walked in the rain.

Skin one alive: stern punishment
My mother will skin me alive if she comes to know that I have not attended college.

SLANG

A slanging match: quarrel in which abusive language is used on both sides
They indulged in a slanging match when the teacher walked into the classroom.

SLEEP

Cry oneself to sleep: weep till you sleep

She would cry herself to sleep every night after her husband left her.

Put someone to sleep: help someone sleep with an anaesthetic.
He was put to sleep before the surgery was conducted.

Put an animal to sleep: kill an animal deliberately when it is very sick or invalid
We put our dog to sleep when he was seventeen years old and sick.

Sleep like a log: in deep slumber
After a hard day's work he sleeps like a log.

Let sleeping dogs lie: not to rake up a problem that is there already
We decided to let sleeping dogs lie and not report to the police.

SLIP

Give somebody the slip: escape
The thief gave the cops a slip in the darkness

A slip of the tongue: blunder of speech
A slip of the tongue cost him the job.

Slip through the fingers: miss an opportunity
She let the opportunity slip through the fingers.

Be slipping: not be alert or cautious
He must be slipping because he has made a lot of mistakes in this report.

SLOW

Slow but steady: unhurried but positive move
He is making slow but steady progress in his studies.

Go slow: go at a sluggish pace
The construction is going on at a very slow pace.

SLY

On the sly: sneakily
We decided to go out of the house on the sly.

SMACK

A smack at something: try to do something
He had a smack at playing golf this summer.

SMALL

Thankful for small mercies: a situation that is better than worse
Let us be thankful for small mercies that the cyclone did not hit our town.

Feel small: be ashamed
When she was pulled up in front of the office staff she felt small and hurt.

A small fortune: expensive
This painting cost us a small fortune.

The small print: parts of a document that can be overlooked
The legal implications of the case are in small print and needs to be studied.

SMELL

Smell a rat: get a feel that something is wrong
She smelt a rat that all was not well inside the house when she entered the gate.

SMOOTH

In smooth waters: steady and easy progress
The construction was in smooth waters till the cyclone set in.

SNAKE

A snake in the grass: untrustworthy or dishonest person who pretends to be a good friend
He is a snake in the grass and is bound to stab you in the back.

SO

So many: innumerable
There are so many stars in the sky.

So much so that: to such an extent that
She liked the painting so much so that she was willing to pay twice the price.

And so on and so forth: continuity in the same fashion
He then described the short comings of the firm and the remedial measures and so on and so forth.

So it be: all right or accepted
If they do not like our play, so it be.

SOLDIER

A soldier of fortune: a person who will serve in any country that will hire him as a soldier or mercenary.
He won the medal of honour as he is a soldier of fortune.

SONG

Song and dance about something: hue and cry over something
There is no need to make a song and dance in this situation.

For a song: sold cheaply or a less price
This piece of painting was sold for a song.

SOON

As soon as: immediately; in a short while
I will come to the hospital as soon as I can.

No sooner said than done: done immediately
You don't have to bother about it—no sooner said than done.

The sooner the better: speedily, as quickly as you can
The sooner you make the decision the better.

Sooner or later: eventually,
Sooner or later he has to abide by the rules of the firm.

SOUR

Turn sour: become bitter or unpleasant
After five years of marriage their love turned sour.

SPANNER

Throw a spanner in the works: spoil the results of someone's hard work
Don't throw a spanner in the works of the children for they have been working on it for long.

SPARE

Spare somebody's feeling: care for a person's feeling
Spare the child's feeling and do not pull him up in front of others.

Spare no pains doing something: try everything possible to achieve something
They spared no pains cleaning the building before the conference was held.

To spare: in excess
We have more than enough food to spare.

Go spare: get angry or upset
Your teacher will go spare when she comes to know that you are not attentive.

Spare somebody's blushes: do not embarrass someone with praises
I hope you will spare my blushes when I am on stage to receive my prize.

SPEAK

Be on speaking terms: friendly terms
I am on speaking terms with the new neighbour.

Nothing to speak: not worthy of mention
The movie is nothing to speak about.

Speak for itself: does not need explaining
The achievement speaks for itself.

Speak for oneself: give out one's opinion
Please speak for youself and do not be influenced by others.

Speak ill of somebody: talk badly about someone
She is always speaking ill of others.

Speak one's mind: express one's opinion frankly
He is known to always speak his mind.

Speak volumes for: depict one's merits
These prizes speak volumes for her talent.

SPILL

Spill the beans: let out a secret
When he was forced by the authorities, he spilt the beans.

Spill blood: cause people to be injured or killed
The fighting sides spilt a lot of blood on either side.

SPIN

Spin one a yarn: tell a sob story to deceive
He will spin a yarn of stories and make the whole class believe in it.

In a flat spin: in a state of panic or confusion
Hearing about the crash the old lady was put in a flat spin.

SPLIT

Split hairs: make very fine demarcations
Do not split hairs, take just the general view.

SPRAT

A sprat to catch a mackerel: a trivial thing that is given up for the sake of getting something bigger.
His offer of a sprat to catch a makerel is unwarranted.

SQUARE

Be square with: even or be in the same level
At any cost he decided to be square with his brother's achievements.

A square meal: sufficient food
She was finding it difficult to have a square meal .

Back to square one: back to the beginning without any progress
We were back to square one when we reached the wrong destination.

A square peg in a round hole: a person whose credentials make him unsuitable for the position.
He felt like a square peg in a round hole when he was asked to do a clerk's job.

STABLE

Lock the stable door when the horse has bolted: become alert after a loss
It is no use locking the stable door when the horse has bolted.

STAND

Take a stand on something: take a decision
We took a stand on the number of students to be admitted to each class.

START

For a start: for the beginning
For a start I would like to introduce you to all the people in the room.

Get off to a good start: begin well or begin successfully
The players got off to a good start in the first half itself.

Start from scratch: come into existence without any help or preparation
We had to start from scratch as all our resources were exhausted in the loss.

To start with: to begin with or firstly
To start with he was only a waiter in a restaurant.

STATE

In a state of affairs: situation
The business is in a sorry state of affairs since the son took over the reigns.

STAY

Be here to stay: be permanent

Liberalisation has come into our country to stay.

Stay put: remain in the same place or position
We had to stay put in the small room till other arrangements were made.

STEAL

Steal the show: get maximum attention or stand out in a show
He stole the show though he was only a newcomer.

STEP

Step into somebody's shoe: stand in place of another person
Only when he stepped into his father's shoe did he realise the responsibilities.

Step on it: go faster
Step on it or you will not get tickets for the show.

Step out of line: react differently or behave differently
The children were punished for stepping out of line.

Step by step: slowly
Step by step they increased the production of all their goods.

Watch one's step: be careful
We have to watch our step each time we stay out late in the nights.

Take steps to do something: find a solution or action
We have to take steps to eradicate poverty in our country.

STICK

Stick in one's mind: remain in one's memory
The movie sticks in the mind of the children for a long time.

Stick one's neck out: take risks
He stuck his neck out to invest in a loss-making enterprise.

STICKY

Sticky fingers: a tendency to steal
She has sticky fingers, so be careful when she comes home.

STING

A sting in the tail: a short-lived good news
The news that a holiday was declared was a sting in the tail as we had to compensate for it on a Sunday.

STINT

Without stint: without any hesitation

She gave away all her money to the orphanage without any stint.

STIR

Stir one's blood: kindle one's feelings
The story will stir your blood and make you want to read more.

Stir one's stumps: hurry up
We had to stir his stumps and make him finish his chores.

STOCK

Out of stock: shortage of supply
The new model of television was out of stock when we went to buy it.

Take stock of something: check the availability or assess
Before we start selling we have to take stock of all the products available.

STOOL

Fall between two stools: fail to choose between two suitable alternatives
She seems uncertain whether she is writing a biography or a narrative, so the writing falls between two stools.

STOP

Stop dead in one's track: stand still or halt suddenly
When I saw the accident in front of my eyes I stopped dead in my tracks.

Stop short of doing something: limit one's actions
She is very cunning but she would definitely stop short of cheating her own sister.

STORM

Take by storm: make a great impact
His speeches have taken the country by storm.

Ride the storm: face a crisis
Though their marriage was opposed by the family they decided to ride the storm together.

Storm in a teacup: uproar over a small matter
People thought that the government would fall after the showdown but it was only a storm in the tea cup.

STRAIGHT

Keep a straight face: have no expressions

When he is talking it is hard to keep a straight face and listen to him.

Put somebody straight: correct somebody's mistake
She decided to put her husband straight by going away for a few days.

Put something straight: put something in order
We decided to put the office straight before the inspection.

STRAW

The final straw: the last event that makes a situation goes out of control
It was the final straw of their marriage when she was seen with another man yet again.

A straw in the wind: inclination of future events
The loss in the company was a straw in the wind that should have warned the management of necessary actions.

Clutch at a straw: having hopes of a unlikely event
He knew that he was clutching a straw when he hoped to marry the girl of his choice.

STRAIN

Strain at the leash: look forward to freedom to do as you please
The final year students are straining at the leash to leave school and have fun.

STRENGTH

Be at full strength: have the required number of people
At the annual general body meeting our team was at full strength to vote in favour of all the decisions.

From strength to strength: slowly increasing in power or success
Her popularity is going from strength to strength as she is very approachable.

STRETCH

Stretch one's legs: relax by walking or moving about
After a long drive we decided to stretch our legs in the open field.

At a stretch: continuously
We sat through two movies at a stretch.

STRIKE

Go on strike: refuse to work

The workers decided to go on strike as there was no hike in their pay.

Strike an attitude: act or pose in a manner which is false
She struck an attitude of devotion to her in-laws though she did not like them.

Strike a balance: find a equilibrium between two extremes
He strikes a fine balance between his work and home.

Strike a blow: make a mark
By her actions she struck a blow against her husband's cruelty.

Strike gold: become rich instantly
He struck gold when he invested in shares.

STRONG

Going strong: keeping the same pace or being active
Though she has crossed sixty she is going srong.

STUFF

A stuffed shirt: high flown or showy person
He is such a stuffed shirt everyone hates him.

SUBLIME

From sublime to the ridiculous: from something admirable or great
From sports to gossip about the film stars, the conversation changed from the sublime to the ridiculous.

SUCH

Such as: for example
Clothes such as these will never suit the occasion.

SUDDEN

All of a sudden: unexpectedly
All of a sudden there was rain and thunderstorm.

SUFFER

Never suffer fools gladly: not to put up with foolish people
My mother never suffers fools gladly and is very strict.

SUIT

Suit one's book: be convenient
It suits my book fine if he decides to visit me tomorrow.

SUN

Under the sun: everything on earth
This is the best place under the sun.

With the sun: early in the morning
She is always up with the sun.

SURE

Be sure to do something: don't miss doing something
Be sure to visit your grandmother this Sunday.

For sure: without any doubt
When I visit your city I will visit the museum for sure.

Sure of oneself: very confident
Though she is new to the school, she is very sure of herself.

Sure enough: certainly
Sure enough the party was a big success.

SUNDRY

All and sundry: each and everyone
He had invited all and sundry to his birthday bash.

SWEEP

Sweep something under the carpet: hide important information
To save his name they swept all his misdeeds under the carpet.

Sweep somebody off his feet: impress someone very much
Her beauty swept him off his feet.

SWALLOW

Swallow one's words: admit one's verbal mistake
I had to swallow my words and tell the teacher about the misbehaviour.

SWEET

At one's own sweet will: at one's pace or time
She finished her assignment at her own sweet will.

Have a sweet tooth: like sweets very much
She has a sweet tooth and can't say no to chocolates.

Sweet nothings: words of love
He wooed her with flowers and sweet nothings.

SWING

Swing into action: deal with the situation quickly
The hospital staff swung into action the minute the ambulance reached the accident site.

Get in the swing: get into a routine
Since he has retired from work it is hard for him to get into the swing.

SYMPATHY

In sympathy with: support a cause
We are all in sympathy with your recent accident.

T

TAB

Keep tabs on something: watch carefully
His parents always keep tabs on all his movements.

TABLE

At table: during meals
We had a big argument at table this morning.

On the table: put out for discussion or consideration
We have left the files on the table for his decisions.

Under the table: not in the open; secretly
A huge sum of money was paid under the table to clinch the deal.

Turn the tables: reverse the position
He lost the previous elections but with his hard work he won this time and turned the tables on his opposition.

TAKE

Take it as it comes: accept a situation when it arises
We have to take life as it comes.

Take it that: assume or think that
I take it that you will attend this evening's party.

Take it upon oneself to do something: decide to do something
He took it upon himself to deal with the police after the robbery.

TAR

Tarred with the same brush: having similar faults
They are all tarred with the same brush and you can expect the same behaviour from them.

TASK

Take someone to task: ridicule someone
When he did not submit his assignment on time he was taken to task by his professor.

TASTE

To taste: gauge the amount required
Add salt to taste.

In bad taste: crude manner
His behaviour at the party was in bad taste in front of all the guests.

TEA

Not for all the tea in China: no matter how great the reward
I wouldn't part with my old car for all the tea in China.

TEAR

Tear something to bits: shred or destroy something
He tore all the documents to bits.

Tear one's hair: show frustration or anger
When the work was not completed on time, he tore his hair in anger.

Be in a tearing hurry: be in a great haste
She was in a tearing hurry to go to the office.

TERMS

Be on good/bad terms: have good or bad relations
He was on good terms with all his colleagues.

Come to terms: make a pact or agreement
We have come to terms with a firm abroad to export our products.

Come to terms with something: reconcile with
You have to come to terms with your loss.

On one's own terms: on one's own conditions
I will sign the agreement only on my own terms.

TEST

Stand the test of time: be stable for a long period of time
These old temples have stood the test of time.

THANK

Have someone to thank: hold someone responsible
I have my mom to thank for our good upbringing.

Thank one's lucky stars: be greatful for one's good luck
He has to thank his lucky stars for being made a manager at such a young age.

THERE

There and back: go back and forth
I think we should go there and be back for dinner.

Then and there: on the spot
He wrote out a cheque for the amount then and there.

THICK

Have a thick head: be foolish or stupid
He has such a thick head that he can never understand any jokes.

As thick as thieves: very close
They are as thick as thieves and you can be sure they will react in the same way.

THIEF

Like a thief in the night: unseen or unexpected
He knocked on my door at night like a thief in the night.

THIN

Have a thin time: be uncomfortable
I had a very thin time at the party last night.

Vanish into thin air: disappear suddenly
I saw her at the reception but after a while she vanished into thin air.

The thin end of the wedge: events that may lead to more important situations
The students regard the principal's intention to ban phones in the college as the thin end of the wedge.

THING

All things considered: all consequences considered
All things considered this is the best route we can take.

As things stand: in the present situation
As things stand he will win the elections hands down.

Be a good thing that: luckily
Be a good thing that you got tickets for this evening's show.

Be seeing things: have wild imaginations
He was seeing things after the road accident.

Do one's own thing: follow one's own interest
He always believes in doing his own thing.

First thing: early in the morning
First thing in the morning I drink a glass of water.

A thing of the past: something that is old or forgotten
These clothes are a thing of the past.

THINK

Think aloud: say what comes to mind
Thinking aloud may land you into a lot of trouble.

Think nothing of it: forget it
We had a fight ten years ago, but think nothing of it and let us start afresh.

Think the world of someone: have very high regards of someone
I think the world of my father.

Put on one's thinking cap: find solutions
Put on your thinking cap and find answers to all these questions.

TIGHT

A tight squeeze: crowded situation
With so many people to eat in the restaurant, it was a tight squeeze.

TILE

On the tiles: having a wild time eating and drinking away from home
The boys were on the tiles after they finished their exams.

TIME

Ahead of time: earlier than expected
The rains came ahead of time.

All the time: throughout
The baby was crying all the time.

At all times: always
He was available to his employees at all times.

At one time: some time in the past
We were the best of friends at one time.

At a time: one after another
We bought all the things in the house one at a time.

Before one's time: in one's past
These paintings have been there before our time.

Every time: always or whenever possible
Everytime he visits us we have a great time.

For the time being: till some alternative is arranged
For the time being we have to live in this small house.

From time to time: every now and then
I get these headaches from time to time.

Give one a hard time: cause suffering to someone
Her in-laws give her a hard time every time she visits them.

Have a good time: enjoy or have fun
We decided to go on a picnic and have a good time.

In no time: quickly
She cooked a tasty meal in no time.

In one's own time: leisurely or in one's spare time
She read the book in her own time.

In time for something: being punctual
We were in time for the play to start.

Move with the times: change according to the present situation
We have to move with the times and change our attitude.

Time and again: repeatedly or again and again
He persuaded her to marry him time and again.

Have the time of one's life: enjoy or make merry
At the party she had the time of her life.

Have time on one's hand: be free or idle
We went out shopping this evening since we had time on our hands.

Time hangs heavy on one's hands: time passes slowly for an idle person
He has retired from work and time hangs heavy on his hands.

TIP

The tip of the iceberg: small part of a complex problem
There have been deaths due to the cold weather but this is just the tip of the iceberg.

Tip the balance: be the deciding factor
His experience tipped the balance in his favour and he got the job.

On the tip of one's tongue: on the verge of uttering something or remembering
His name was on the tip of my tongue but it was too late to call him.

TIRED

Be tired of something: having had enough of something
I am tired of being taken for a ride by you.

Tired out: weak and exhausted
We were tired out trying to find a solution to the problem.

TOFFEE

Can't do something for toffee: does not have a particular skill
He can't sing for toffee.

TOP

At the top of the tree: reach the highest position in one's career or profession
At a very young age he has reached the top of the tree.

At thc top of one's voice: very loudly
The teacher was shouting at the top of her voice at the noisy children.

From top to bottom: from beginning to end
We looked for the lost dairy from top to bottom.

On top: be in control
Throughout the competition she was on top of the list.

Feel on top of the world: feel elated or very happy
I feel on top of the world since the time I met him.

Over the top: too much without limits
He has gone over the top with his drinking habit.

TOUCH

Touch the right cord: make a good impact
She always touched the right cord with all her seniors.

At a touch: tapped or touched lightly
This machine works at a touch.

Out of touch: not in use of something
I am out of touch with writing letters and it is difficult to correspond.

TOUGH

Get tough with one: be strict or firm
She decided to get tough with her wayward son.

A tough customer: not easy to please
She is a tough customer when it comes to choosing her clothes.

TRACK

In one's tracks: suddenly, instantly
When we saw the accident we just stopped in our tracks.

Keep track of something: be in touch with something
We have to keep track of the political developments in the country.

On the right track: following the right directions
We were on the right track throughout the journey.

TREAT

Treat one like dirt: disrespect someone or ill treat someone
When he went to ask for money he was treated like dirt by his relatives.

TRIAL

Stand trial: tested and tried in court of law
She has to stand trial for her misconduct in the company.

On trial: being tested
This product was introduced on trial for one week.

Trial and error: test and find out the flaws
We are following these instructions on a trial and error basis.

TRICK

Be up to one's old tricks: act in the usual unpleasant manner

Once he returned home he is up to his old tricks.

Every trick in the book: all possible methods to achieve the result
He used every trick in the book to mend his son's behaviour.

Have a trick up one's sleeve: plan of action, or idea
He had a trick up his sleeve when he went to sell his product.

The tricks of the trade: expert ways to deal with business
He was successful as he was very sure of all the tricks of the trade.

TROUBLE

Get into trouble: get oneself into problems or nuisance
She got into trouble when she got into an argument with the shopkeeper.

Give one trouble: cause problems
Her son always gives her lots of trouble.

In trouble: be in difficulty
He is in trouble financially.

Take trouble over something: take extra effort in doing something
We took a lot to trouble over finding an appropriate gift for him.

TRUE

Come true: really happen
His dreams have finally come true.

One's true colours: one's real character
When he was approached to donate some money he showed his true colours.

True to something: be the real self
True to her good reputation, she donated money to the orphanage.

TRY

Try one's hand at something: attempt something
I am trying my hand at snorkelling these days.

Try one's luck: have a go or shot at something
We have to try our luck at the casino tonight.

TUNE

In tune with something: in accordance with something
These clothes are sewn in tune with the designs given.

To the tune of something: amounting to
She lost assets to the tune of fifty lakhs.

TURN

As things turned out: as things happened
As things turned we did not have any problems clinching the deal.

Be well turned out: be well dressed or have a good appearance
We must teach our children to be well turned out.

At every turn: all the time
He had to struggle at every turn of his career.

Do one a good turn: be helpful
He decided to do her a good turn when she was in difficulties.

In turn: one after another
We decided to stay at home in turns.

Out of turn: at a very inappropriate time
He gets into trouble for always talking out of turn.

A turn of events: change of scene or new developments
The turn of events in this case has given us lots of hopes.

The turn of the year: when the New Year begins
At the turn of this year we will make a resolution to stay fit.

TURTLE

Turn turtle: turn upside down
The boat we were riding in turned turtle before we jumped out.

TWIST

Twist one's arm: be forceful
He had to twist the guard's arm in order to gain entry into the building.

Twist one round one's finger: be able to influence someone
The little girl twisted her parents round her little finger and got away with all mischief.

TWITTER

All of a twitter: be on the edge or nervous
The students were all of a twitter on the day of the results.

TWO

In twos and threes: two or three at a time
We were allowed into the stadium in twos and threes.

In a day or two: in a few days
We will visit you in a day or two.

Put two and two together: add up to or make a guess taking the clues
We put two and two together and found that she was not interested in the business.

That makes two of us: being in the same position as one
"I am having difficulty understanding this problem." "That makes two of us."

U

UGLY

An ugly customer: unpleasant person to deal with
He is an ugly customer and is never welcome in our office.

An ugly duckling: is not very pleasing to look at
She was an ugly duckling until she learnt how to groom herself.

UMBRAGE

Take umbrage at something: feel offended
The teacher took umbrage at the child's remarks and punished him.

UNAWARES

Catch somebody unawares: take someone by surprise
He was caught unawares when he was stealing in the store.

UNCERTAIN

In no uncertain terms: make things very clear
We stated in no uncertain terms what we had against the manager.

UNCROWNED

Uncrowned king/queen of something: leader in a particular field
He is the uncrowned king of golfing these days.

UNDERSTAND

Give someone to understand that: cause someone to think
We were given to understand that the principal will not be available today.

UNDERSTANDING

On the understanding that: on the condition that
We let this place out on the understanding that we get a good rent.

UNDIVIDED

Have one's individed attention: concentrate fully
You have my undivided attention.

UNKNOWN

An unknown quantity: unpredictable amount/person
The new team leader is still an unknown quantity.

Unknown to somebody: without the knowledge of somebody
Quite unknown to me, she has booked the tickets.

UNSOUND

Of unsound mind: insane
He is of unsound mind and should not be taken seriously.

UP

Be up to somebody: desired or required to be
It is up to the children to take care of their aged parents.

Be up with something: be unwell
She seems to be up with some ache or the other.

Up against something: face some difficulty or problem
He is up against corrupt officials who will create trouble for him.

Up and about: being normal after an illness or injury
He is up and about after a bout of flu.

Up and down: forwards and backwards
We went up and down the street but could not locate the store.

Up to something: plotting something or busy with something
Do not disturb him he is up to some serious work in his room.

Ups and downs: highs and lows or good or bad luck
There are many ups and downs in life which we have to face.

UPPER

Get an upper hand: get control of a situation
We should not let our enemies get an upper hand in this deal.

The upper crust: high class society or the elite people
The party was meant only for the upper crust of the society.

USE

Come into use: be helpful or come in handy
When will this tool come into use?

Have no use for something: have no purpose
We have no use for furniture like this in our house.

Make use of something: put something into use
We have to make use of all the resources that we have got.

USEFUL

Make oneself useful: help by performing useful tasks
My nephews tried to make themselves useful about the house.

USUAL

As usual: normal or routine
He was late as usual for the show.

V

VACUUM

In a vacuum: isolated
He prefers to work in a vacuum throughout the day.

VAIN

In vain: fruitless or without any result
We tried in vain to stop him from leaving the country.

VENGEANCE

With a vengeance: furiously or forcefully
The rain came down with a vengeance.

VENT

Give vent to something: outlet or pour out
He gave vent to his anger on his children.

VERGE

On the verge of something: on the brink or just about to
He was on the verge of resigning his job when he got a raise.

VEST

Having a vested interested: benefit from
He has a vested interest in those shares as a major part of his savings has gone to them.

VEX

A vexed question: a controversial or problem-causing question
It is a vexed question as to who will become the next prime minister.

VICIOUS

A vicious circle: a chain of events that is the cause and effect in itself
Taking or giving a bribe will give rise to a vicious circle of corruption.

VICTIM

Fall victim to something: succumb to
She fell victim to the charm of the manager.

VIEW

Have something in view: have a clear-cut plan or intention
We have to make plans having our strengths and weaknesses in view.

In my view: in my opinion
In my view this is not the right direction to his house.

In view of something: considering
In view of bad light we have to start the game early.

VIRTUE

By virtue of something: because of something
By virtue of his good nature, he was able to win many friends in a short time.

Make a virtue of necessity: do something in good faith
Keeping ill health, I made virtue of necessity and gave up smoking.

VOGUE

Come into vogue: be in fashion
Short dresses have come into vogue due to the weather.

VOLITION

Of one's own volition: of one's own free will
She left the house of her own volition.

W

WAGON

On the wagon: become a teetotaler or give up alchohol
After his health worsened he is now on the wagon.

WAIT

Keep someone waiting: delay someone
It is not good manners to keep someone waiting.

Wait and see: observe before reacting
We have to wait and see if his health will improve.

Wait at table: serve food and drinks at a restaurant.
When he was a student he had to wait at tables to pay his fees.

A waiting game: a deliberate delay in acting
He is sick and tired of the waiting game she is playing before giving her consent.

WAKE

Wake the dead: be very loud
His voice was loud enough to wake the dead.

One's waking hours: the time when one is awake
In his waking hours he manages to finish all his work effortlessly.

In the wake of something: as a consequence of something
In the wake of political unrest, the country was reduced to poverty.

WALK

Run before one can walk: try to master difficult tasks before knowing the basics.
In your career never run before you can walk.

A walking dictionary: having a very good vocabulary or usage of words.
She is a walking dictionary and she will win this competition hands down.

Walk one's leg off: walk till you are exhausted
She decided to walk her legs off to reach the destination in time.

Walk tall: feel confident
After we won the match we were able to walk tall.

A walk of life: occupation of career
During our trip to the north we met people from all walks of life.

WALL

To the wall: to a difficult situation
He was pushed to the wall by his seniors so that he would resign in desperation.

Up the wall: angry or crazy
He is always driving his mother up the wall.

WAR

At war: in a state of battle
Our neighbouring countries have been at war for years now.

Have been in the wars: scars of war or ill treatment
He has been in the wars and his behaviour tells us so.

A war of words: verbal insult or abuse
She got into a war of words with her mother-in-law.

WARPATH

Go on a warpath: ready for battle or fight
When it comes to the question of equal rights, she is the first one to be on the warpath.

WARM

Keep somebody's seat warm: temporarily occupy somebody's seat
She kept her sister's seat warm for six months till she returned from abroad.

WASH

Wash one's dirty linen in public: openly discuss a personal matter
Our neighbours are known to wash their dirty linen in public.

Wash one's hands off something: have nothing to do with a particular thing
She decided to wash her hands off all her official responsibilities.

WATCH

Keep watch: guard or keep vigil
They kept watch on the towers in turns.

Watch it: be careful
Watch it, don't go out during the night.

Watch the clock: not to work more than the required time
The workers in the factory would never watch the clock to complete their task.

Watch this space: wait for further news regarding a particular announcement.
Watch this space for more schemes to be announced.

Watch the time: keep track of the clock or time
He would always watch the time and be in time for all his appointments.

Watch the world go by: keep track of the latest developments around one
The old invalid lady used to sit by the window and watch the world go by.

WATER

By water: travel by boat or ship
We decided to travel to the island by water.

Like water: lavishly or recklessly
The teenagers were spending money like water at the club.

Much water has flowed under the bridge: many things have happened since
Much water has flowed under the bridge since you left the country five years ago.

WAY

All the way: the whole distance
She came all the way to meet the whole family.

Be set in one's ways: very firm and rigid in one's thinking

He is so set in his way that it is hard for him to adjust to anyone.

By the way: by the roadside
We stopped for picnic by the way.

By way of: with the help
We helped children in the orphanage by way of donating clothes.

Come one's way: happen or occur to a person
Good luck seems to have come his way this year.

Have one's own way: do as one wishes with or without opposition
She believes in having her own way in everything she does.

Give way: collapse or break down
The old bridge gave way and the bus plunged into the water.

Give way to something: be replaced by something
The narrow roads gave way to green fields.

Go out of one's way: take great pains or care to do something
He will go out of his way to help the needy.

In a bad way: very sick
He is laid up in bad in a bad way.

In a way: to a certain extent
In a way she seems to have sent a bad message across to her family.

In the way: obstructing
Her husband is coming in the way of her career.

Make way for someone or something: let go or allow to pass
We had to make way for the dignitaries to pass by first .

One way or the other: somehow or by some method
We will solve this problem one way or the other.

On the way out: as you exit or while going out
Please switch off the lights on the way out!

The other way round: reversed
We expected the show to be slow and dull but it turned out to be the other way round.

Out of the way: very far
He lives out of the way from our house.

Stand in someone's way: prevent someone from doing something
He would always stand in the way of her pursuing her hobbies.

Ways and means: methods and devices to do things
There are lots of ways and means to reach one's goals

Have a way with: have the capacity to convince
He has a way with words and can easily sell anything.

WEAK

Weak at the knees: emotionally powerless
I went weak at the knees on hearing his proposal.

Weak in the head: dull or stupid
She was so weak in the head that she decided to leave school.

A weak moment: a delicate or tempting moment
In a weak moment she relented to his proposal.

WEATHER

In all weather: during all seasons or climate
The buses will commute in all weather.

Under the weather: feeling ill or unwell
I was under the weather throughout the morning

WEIGH

Weigh a ton: very heavy
The books weighed a ton in this small bag

Weigh one's words: be careful with what you say
Weigh your words before you talk to little children.

WEIGHT

Lose weight: become less heavy
We decided to lose weight by exercising.

Take the weight off one's feet: sit down
Late in the evening she took the weight off her feet and rested for an hour.

WELL

All well and good: satisfactory
This project report has been made all well and good.

As well: along with or in addition to
She is a good cook as well as a good painter.

Do well: be successful
She decided to study hard and do well in her exams this time.

Very well: an expression used to give consent
Very well, you may use my car for the weekend.

Well aware: fully informed or updated
We are well aware of all the dangers of this trip.

Well off: rich or financially sound
Her husband is well off and she need not work the whole day.

WET

Wet behind the ears: inexperienced
She is still wet behind the ears to handle such a big business.

A wet blanket: be a spoilt sport
He turned out to be such a wet blanket at the New Year party.

Wet through: soaked
We were wet through the journey as we were caught in the rain.

Wet one's whistle: have a drink
After the success of the project the team decided to wet their whistle at the restaurant.

WHALE

Have a whale of a time: enjoy or make merry
We had a whale of a time at the birthday party.

WHEEL

Behind the wheel: driving
He wanted to get behind the wheels and teach her how to drive correctly.

Wheels within wheels: confusing or complicated situations that is difficult to understand.
Our political systems are wheels within wheels which is not in the reach of common man.

Wheel and deal: intelligent bargain
We have to wheel and deal a good amount of discount before buying the product.

WHIP

Have the whip hand: be in control
He has the whip hand in running the business.

WHIRL

Give something a whirl: experiment with something
We decided to give snorkelling a whirl though we do not know anything about it.

WHISKER

By a whisker: by a very small margin or difference
We missed the accident by a whisker.

WHITE

White as a sheet: pale after a shock or fear
She was white as a sheet when she witnessed the accident.

As white as snow: very white; the colour of snow
This sheet of paper is as white as snow.

A white elephant: something very expensive to maintain
The new car is only a white elephant and cannot be used regularly.

WHOLE

Go the whole hog: do a task thoroughly.
After researching for so long he decided to go the whole hog and conduct the experiment.

The whole bag of tricks: collection of things or fun things to do
The magician had a whole bag of tricks to keep the children entertained.

A whole lot of: a large number of
She has a whole lot of clothes that she never wears.

As a whole: as one unit
She preferred to buy the cardboard sheets as a whole to make boxes.

On the whole: considering everything
On the whole he is a very likeable person.

WIDE

Fall wide off the mark: be far away from the actual point or goal
His arrows fell wide off the mark in the competition.

Give somebody a wide berth: keep a safe distance from someone
Knowing what a cunning person he is I always give him a wide berth.

Wide open: could be anyone's game
The contest was wide open till the last round was played.

Wide awake: alert
The sentry was wide awake throughout the night.

WILD

Beyond one's wildest dreams: better than what was expected
The success of the play was beyond our wildest dreams.

Run wild: roam about freely
After working hard through the week he runs wild over the weekends.

WILL

Against one's will: against one's wishes
I went to the party against my will.

At will: as and when one desires
Visitors moved about in the exhibition at will

With a will: enthusiastically or eagerly
We must put our minds to learning and study with a will.

WIN

Win one's spurs: achieve fame
He won his spurs with his first painting exhibition.

Win or lose: gain or lose
Win or lose we have to put our best in this endeavour.

WIND

Get one's second wind: feel relaxed or refreshed
She got her second wind when all the children went home for the day.

Like the wind: very fast
He ran like the wind to reach the bus stop in time.

Take the wind out of somebody's sails: cause someone to lose his confidence or pride
He took the wind out of her sails when he fired her from the job.

To the four winds: scattered in all directions
The dried leaves have blown to the four winds on the street.

Winds of change: tendency to change
She has introduced winds of change in the office.

Get the wind of something: get an early clue or warning
We got the wind of his uncouth behaviour even before he joined the firm.

In the winds: about to happen or take place
From the gossip in the office alot of changes are in the winds.

WINE

Wine and dine: entertain with food and drink
They had to wine and dine the client before they struck the deal.

WING

Wait in the wings: ready to do or take over from somebody
He is waiting in the wings for his senior to retire.

On the wing: flying
She is always on the wing as she is the pilot's wife.

WINK

Take forty winks: have a short nap
I enjoy taking forty winks every afternoon .

Bstay awake
She could not sleep a wink due to a bad headache.

WIPE

Wipe the floor with somebody: defeat someone decisively in a competition
We wiped the floor with the best team.

Wipe something off the face of the earth: destroy something completely
Our government is working towards wiping polio off the face of the earth.

Wipe the slate clean: forget the past and restart a new life
She wiped the slate clean and decided to live life after her husband's death.

WISE

Get wise to someone or something: become aware or realise
After meeting the man she became wise to his charming ways.

None the wiser: knowing no more than earlier
We have become none the wiser even after so many defeats in the matches.

Wise as an owl: full of wisdom
The old woman is wise as an owl.

WISH

As you wish: as you desire
You can deal with the problem as you wish.

Wish someone or something well: hope that something fortunate will happen
We wished him well in his new venture.

WIT

At one's wits end: not knowing what to do or say because of worry

She's at wits end worrying that her kids have not returned home from school.

Gather one's wit: recover from a shock
After the accident she gathered her wits and called her family.

Wit and wisdom: combination of intelligence and humour.
The stories she narrated were filled with lots of wit and wisdom.

WOLF

Keep the wolf from the door: have enough money to avoid hunger and need
They are so poor that they can hardly keep the wolf from the door.

A wolf in sheep's clothing: a person who appears harmless but isn't
He was a wolf in sheep's clothing and she believed him.

Throw somebody to the wolves: being thrown open to a harsh reality
When she joined the new college she felt like she was being thrown to the wolves.

WONDER

It's a wonder that: its surprising that
It's a wonder that she is able to finish the assignment so quickly

WOOD

From the wood: from the wooden barrel
They drank beer from the wood.

Not see the wood for the trees: not understanding the main point
If you mark your copy so lightly, we will not be able to see the wood for the tree.

Out of the woods: out of danger
After treatment for six months, she is finally out of the woods.

WORD

At the word of command: when an order is given
The soldiers fired at the word of command

Be as good as one's word: keep one's promise
You can depend on her to be as good as her word.

Be not the word for somebody: inadequate description of somebody
Miser is not the word for him! He is tight fisted.

By word of mouth: by talk or spoken words
His paintings were sold only by word of mouth.

Give somebody one's word: promise somebody
I have given her my word that the assignment will be completed in one month.

Go back on one's word: not keep one's promise
They went back on their word that the furniture will be delivered the next day.

Have a word with somebody: speak to someone in private
The teacher wanted to have a word with me regarding my son.

Have words: quarrel
She had words with her father and walked out of the house.

Not a word: don't say anything
Not a word was said to anyone about the new scheme.

Put in a word: recommend
He put in word to his friends about the sale of books.

Put words in somebody's mouth: speak for someone else
She accused the manager of putting words in her mouth.

Take somebody's word for it: accept something on a person's authority.
I'll take your word for it that this mistake will not be repeated again.

Take the words right out of somebody's mouth: say exactly what the other person was about to say
She took the words right out of his mouth and rejected the proposal.

Too funny for words: very witty that is cannot be expressed
The new movie is too funny for words.

Without a word: quietly or silently
She walked out of the room without a word.

Word for word: verbatim
Can you repeat it word for word?

Somebody's word is as good as his bond: a person's promise is very reliable
His word is as good as his bond you, so can easily trust him.

One's word of honour: a promise
Come what may you can rely on his word of honour.

A word to the wise: a person who can intelligently take a hint and act accordingly

A word to the wise is enough to make them understand any difficult situation.

WORK

At work: place of work
He was cheated very badly at work.

At work on something: busy with something
Please do not disturb him while he is at work with the experiments.

Get down to work: start or begin a task or errand
We have had a lot of fun now, let us get down to work seriously.

Go about one's work: keep doing one's work
After the party she went about her work of clearing up the place.

Good works: acts of charity
She won an award for her good works.

Out of work: without a job
He was out of work for more than a year.

Set somebody to work: make someone start working on something
We set the team to work on the new project.

The work of a moment: the job that take a specific time
It was the work of a moment to finish the filing the papers.

Work it/things: arrange matters
Work things in such a way that we get some free time in the evenings.

WORKING

In working order: running in smooth condition
All the machines in the factory are in working order.

WORLD

Mean the world to somebody: mean everything to somebody
My grandchildren mean the world to me.

Come up in the world: become more important in the society
They are coming up in the world in spite of stiff competition.

For the world: whatever the return is
I will not give up this profession for the world.

In a world on one's own: live in an imaginative world
He missed the route as he was in a world of his own.

A man/woman of the world: an experienced person
She is a woman of this world and she will give you a good advice.

Out of this world: wonderful or beautiful
The clothes displayed in the shop are out of this world.

The outside world: people or places outside a particular community or group
Only when you go into the outside world will you know what life is.

The world in one's oyster: one is able to enjoy all the pleasures of life
He left home with the idea that the world was in his oyster.

A world of difference: a great deal of difference
Change of school has made a world of difference to the child.

Be worlds apart: be completely different
They are brothers but are worlds apart in character and conduct.

The world over: everywhere
The world over there was a threat to peace.

Set the world on fire: achieve great fame
He set the world on fire with his latest invention.

WORRY

Not to worry: do not worry or fret
We have run into debt, but not to worry—we can tide over it very soon.

WORSE

Worse luck: bad luck or unfortunate luck
They have to leave their jobs, worse luck!

Be worse off: be unhappier or poorer than before
After the famine all the farmers are worse off.

Go from bad to worse: deteriorate
His health condition has gone from bad to worse in three weeks.

Be none the worse for something: be unharmed
The motorists were none the worse for their journey in the woods.

Make matters worse: make the situation even more difficult
She made matters worse by leaving the job in a hurry.

WORST

At the worst: something more unpleasant
At the worst he will have to stay up the night to finish his homework.

Do one's worst: be as difficult or unpleasant as possible.
She decided to do her worst when she did not get her way in the decision making.

If the worst comes to the worst: if a situation goes even bad than it already is
If worst comes to worst we will have to sell our property to pay back the loans.

WORTH

For all one is worth: with all one's effort
We needed his help, so we cajoled him for all we were worth.

For what it's worth: the value of something
We have to take care of the jewels for what it's worth.

Not worth a damn: useless
Their opinions are not worth a damn.

Worth it: efforts being paid back
We were able to clinch the deal after four months and it was worth it.

Worth its weight in gold: extremely important or useful
His advice is worth its weight in gold

Worth somebody's while: interesting to someone
It would be worth your while to check your purse before you leave.

WRAP

Be wrapped in something: be covered up in something
The whole box is wrapped up in paper and it is hard to find out what it contains.

Wrap somebody up in cotton wool: protect someone from any dangers
She wrapped her kids in cotton wool and they are not able to face the world now.

Under wraps: secret
The whole episode was kept under wraps from the public eye.

WRING

Wring one's hands: twist one's hand with worry
She was wringing her hands in fear for her child had not returned home.

Wring someone's neck: strangle someone's neck
Once he comes to know who did this he will wring their neck in anger.

WRITE

Be written all over one's face: very obvious
She can never tell a lie, it is written all over her face.

WRITING

In writing: in a written form
He wanted her statement in writing.

The writing is on the wall: clear signs or signals of failure
The writing is on the wall for her and she has to leave soon.

WRONG

On the wrong side of the tracks: living in an area considered inferior socially
Since he was living on the wrong side of the track, she did not accept his proposal.

Get somebody wrong: misunderstand someone
Do not get me wrong, I did not mean to hurt you.

Go wrong: make a mistake
Anyone can go wrong in dealing with money.

In the wrong: being responsible for a mistake
There is no doubt that she is in the wrong in their relationship.

Y

YEAR

All the year round: throughout the year
We had rains all the year round.

Man/woman of the year: outstanding person of the year
She was chosen the woman of the year and she deserves it.

Not in a hundred years: never
Not in a hundred years can I trust him.

Put years on somebody: make someone appear aged or older
The hard work and stress has put years on him.

Take years off somebody: make someone appear younger
The new haircut has taken years off her face.

Year after year: every year
He made donations to the orphanage year after year.

Year by year: progressing year
The size of the organisation grew year by year.

The year dot: long time ago
He made a name for himself from the year dot.

Year in and year out: each and every year
We went to the same location year in and year out.

Year of grace: any specified year after the birth of Christ.
In the year of grace of 1988, polio was eradicated from this world.

YELLOW

A yellow streak: a coward
Though he seems to be brave, he has a yellow streak in him.

YET

As yet: until now
We have not seen the photographs as yet.

Yet again: once more
He was caught in the act of bribing yet again.

YOUNG

Not so young as one used to be: getting older
I cannot run fast, I am not as young as I used to be.

Not get any younger: become old
You cannot walk all the way up, you are not getting any younger.

Young and old: all, regardless of age
This is an occasion for the young and old to meet.

Young at heart: feel young but physically old
He is young at heart but his body is not listening.

Be with the young: pregnant
She is with the young and needs medical help.

YOURSELF

By yourself: alone without help
She drove all the way by herself.